CARRYING WATER as a Way of Life

A Homesteader's History

Linda Tatelbaum

About Time Press
Appleton, Maine

Printed by J. S. McCarthy, Augusta, Maine, USA

Cover Design by Ribeck & Co.
Cover Illustration by Chris Van Dusen
Photos by Bonnie Farmer
Logo Design by Noah T. Winer and Fred Ribeck

Typeset by Grace Von Tobel in New Century Schoolbook
font on a Macintosh Performa 636 using
Adobe Pagemaker 6.0

ISBN 0-9654428-0-2
Library of Congress Catalog Card Number 96-96938

Fifth Printing

About Time Press
1050 Guinea Ridge Road
Appleton, Maine 04862
207-785-4634

For Kal

who loves the place as much as I do

and for Noah

"the apple doesn't fall far from the tree"

Thank you

To Kalman Winer and Noah Tatelbaum Winer, for
   living it with me.
To Harriet and Milton Tatelbaum and Harold Winer,
   for believing in me.
To Tobin Simon and Linda Trichter-Metcalf, for pushing me.
To Kate Barnes, for praising me.
To Jean Donovan Sanborn, for reading me.
To David and Anne Emerson, for helping us build.
To Marta Cardarelli and the late Joe, for loving the place.
To friends, who came to live and garden in this neck of the woods,
   and stayed.
To Fred Ribeck, Gail Whitaker Ribeck, Judy Daviau,
   Grace Von Tobel, Bonnie Farmer, Chris Van Dusen
   and Colby College for assistance.

Some of these essays have appeared previously: "Jars" in *Farmstead*; "Carrying Water as a Way of Life" in *Countryside*; "A Homesteader's History" in *Harrowsmith* and *Harrowsmith Country Reader*; "For Love or Money," "12 Ways of Looking at Trash," "The Language of the Trees," "The Rockland That Was" in *Maine Times*; "Down to the Wire," "Power of Choice," "The Old Well," and "Even Stones Dissolve in the Rain" in *Maine Sunday Telegram*.

Preface

Lesson in Eco-nomics

1996

It's an economic story.

I never would have said so back in the days of rusted red Volkswagen, faded pink trailer parked under milkweed in an overgrown field. To build a house, to plant a garden, to make a life—self-sufficient, simple. I didn't understand, in 1977, how deeply a homesteader's history is rooted in the economic forces that surround her. How deeply anyone's history.

I would have said it was aesthetics, philosophy, botany. I would have called it poetry, back in the kerosene lamp days, the hauling water days. I would have claimed to be putting down roots and bringing forth greens, making a life.

But really, it comes down to making a living: negotiating the complex dynamic between people, land, money, work. Between me, home, income, career.

> Making do vs. doing without,
> doing-it-yourself vs. hiring it out,
> growing your own vs. buying it,
> working at home vs. "working out"

—which used to mean going off the farm to work, not weight-lifting, though I suppose it amounts to the same thing. Building muscle, discipline, character, endurance.

I still say it's not only about money, this story. It's about saving something besides money. Save time save the planet save face save water save space save the whales save the children save scraps save seeds save energy

save your breath .

just do what you can

Résumé

A Homesteader's History

Linda Tatelbaum
Burkettville, Maine

Born February 28, 1947   *Rochester, New York*

1965: Graduate, Brighton High School, Rochester, New York.

1968: B.A., Cornell University, Ithaca, New York, in Romance Languages & Literature.

1969: M.A., Cornell University, in Medieval Studies.

1972: PhD., Cornell University, in Medieval Literature & Philology.

I join the glut of new PhD's, 200 of us vying for every tenure-track opening at American colleges and universities. By the skin of my teeth, I get a position as Assistant Professor at a college no one's ever heard of. The good news is, I get to live in New Hampshire.

1974: The college goes bankrupt. Watergate bursts open. The Arab oil crisis hits home, and I can't pay my oil bill. With my good friend the dean of students, I decide to drop out, do physical labor, earn my keep on this planet for a change. I barter my labor on a farm for cordwood, cow's milk, maple syrup, old canning jars. I will never need money again, or "good clothes," or anything made of plastic, or light bulbs, extension cords, ice cube trays, books that aren't "how-to" manuals. Good-bye to all that.

We live in a one-room cabin my ex-dean built by hand in the woods. We eat from wooden bowls, drink from stoneware mugs, use chopsticks. Nothing metal or plastic or china will ever touch our lips again. No alarm clocks, radios. No newspapers except to start the cookstove. We eat beans and rice, vegetables, yogurt, whole wheat bread. The seasons rule us. We are one with the woods.

1975: I marry my woods-companion. I chop wood and carry water. He operates a lathe from 9 to 5 at a factory in town, and comes home grey.

1976: We join the glut of back-to-the-landers swayed by *The Mother Earth News* into believing that somewhere in Appalachia there's a farmhouse and land where we can be happy homesteaders. In six months, we're back in New Hampshire, living in a motel and looking for jobs. We find them, and a small rented house with a garden. We raise our own food, save all our money, and start looking for land where there's plenty of winter.

1977: We buy 75 acres in Maine and build our own house, plant a garden. We use only hand tools, including the two-person crosscut saw which nearly destroys but ultimately improves our marriage.

1979: I am pregnant. The nurse says I must drink milk, eat liver and fish once a week. I have no refrigerator and don't want to break my vows of simplicity, but disregarding her advice fills me with doubt. Two weeks before delivery, I go into a discount store and stand, bewildered, in front of rows of consumer products— Kleenex, baby wipes, ointments. I feel I've re-entered a world I once knew and rejected. I spend $20 on things not made by hand. The baby comes, hospital delivered. I change his cloth diapers by flashlight at night; I lug a bushel basket of diapers to the laundromat every week; I haul water while baby sleeps; I grind grain for his pablum, and cook it on a woodstove. I am exhausted. I want my mother, or canned soup, or baseboard heat. Or do I? At least if I could switch on a light when baby cries at 2 a.m., not fumble with a kerosene lamp while milk leaks down my chest and baby howls. At least if I didn't have to go down cellar everytime he wants apple juice. At least if I had a drain, so I didn't have to lug water in *and* out. At least if my mother could come and I didn't have to write her a manual for how to boil water on the woodstove for a cup of tea. I'm so tired.

1981: I go back to work as a professor, part-time. I get up in the dark and eat breakfast by kerosene light. Dressed up in my new clothes, I haul water, trying not to perspire or spill water on my stockings. Our dirt road is the last in town to get plowed, so I leave extra early in snow, and then mud, to make the hour commute for an 8 o'clock class. I read student papers by Aladdin lamplight at night. At the college I feel like a creature from another planet, until I find out my colleague in the next office, who had me fooled with his three-piece suit, lives in a log cabin and has to ski out to his car in the dark each morning. I begin to see how funny it all is.

1983: We build an addition with a bedroom for our son, a study for me. We install photovoltaics to power lights and a water pump. We put in a drain. We get a 12" black-and-white TV. Our friends are shocked. They are homesteaders, too, but they have long since put in power, washing machines, freezers, taken jobs in town, and they regret to see us change. We are the last "pure" homesteaders around. They want us to die for their sins. But we want to live, and not just subsist. I begin to write again, seriously, in the time gained not hauling water and filling the lamps.

1987: Ten years on the land, and I still garden, I still eat homegrown food, I still cook on a woodstove. But I do buy bananas and an occasional fresh broccoli in winter. I still make my own yogurt and bread, but I don't grind my own flour with a hand mill any-more. I still eat from my same wooden bowl, but I do like wine in a stemmed glass or setting the table with my grandmother's china once in awhile. I still live on the same rutted narrow dirt road, but now I drive a recent-model four-wheel-drive Toyota to my job at the college, no longer an old Volks. I still walk in the woods for enter-tainment, but I do like TV and going out to dinner. I still like to watch my son growing up close to nature, but I do cook him hot dogs and let him buy gum sometimes.

I don't *want* to make my own Grape-Nuts or grow my own mustard seed! I've stopped reading *Mother Earth News* and other back-to-the-land magazines that extol the "simple life." Call it enough to eat from the garden year 'round. Call it enough to be minimally responsible for the world's pollution. There's work to do "out there," human-to-human work, and if I'm home hauling water uphill from my spring and ekeing out a living from the soil, how can the world be served? After all, even woodsmoke from my two stoves is an air pollutant, and my solar electric panels are made from silicone, copper, plastic, rubber. I'll never be pure unless I go live in a cave and wear animal skins. But then I'd have to kill animals, wouldn't I?

I've come to believe in compromise. I believe that conforming to anything warps a life, that keeping up with the Nearings is just another form of rat-race. So watch out, because as soon as we've saved enough money, we're getting hot water.

1988: We got it, hot water, a kitchen cookstove that burns wood or propane, and one last addition to the house: a dining room with a glass door. This is as modern as we'll ever get, we say.

1990: Until we buy the leather couch. Now we approach the post-modern primitive, living with animal skins after all, in a com-fortable cave that's "off the grid." Our cave now has a color TV and a computer in it, run by solar electricity. Photovoltaics cost money, don't think they don't, almost as much as the 17 acres across the road that we grab from developers by taking out our very first bank loan. This is more modern than we ever wanted to get.

We still grow our own food, and I still do canning, 300 quarts a year. We buy wood, despite the fact that we now own 92 acres. There's only so much time.

1993: We haven't moved, but town is getting closer than ever. The trip to the High School takes half-an-hour each way, and our son's life happens there now. A major corporation moves into that coastal town and pushes it well into "the 90s," with balsamic vinaigrette and sourdough bread easily available where ten years ago there was scarcely a bagel. A good old Bean Supper gets harder to find, but the best one still happens at the Grange in our little hamlet. People who can't afford the booming real estate prices on the coast start buying land in this neck of the woods. There are now nine families living on this one-lane dirt road.

1995: We add two more solar panels to our photovoltaic array, bringing us to 18. Now we have two computers and three phones. But don't worry: no answering machine. Home remains the cave where we can hold "the world" out, sort of. We still produce a cellar full of food and prefer to stay home and eat it. A new century looms as our son prepares to leave.

1977

K. Winer

THE PLACE

"For years we've been making our home..
All we needed was a place to put it."

—*Diary entry, 10/25/77*

House
excerpts from a diary

1977

5/1 We're HERE, on our land in Maine, a pink trailer for a home. "Pinkie" is old and has been around, with many views from its windows. The view now is mine, poplars, milkweed, an ancient overgrown grapevine. Here to stay. I sit by kerosene light and write my three sentences a day (or 2, or 4), an album, a record, not a fiction.

6/18 I have mixed feelings about the work, the life, of being here. At times I feel pride and awe that I, who can work w/ my mind, live here now, working w/ my body. And yet I'm still chafing against the restraints. So much of your life you spend preparing, so that looking to the future becomes a habit of mind, & it's hard to realize that THIS IS IT, this is your life: now get to work.

7/1 John finally came with backhoe and bulldozer to dig the cellar. I cried to see what destruction our creativity brings to this land.

7/8 Cement trucks here all day for "the pour." Housebuilding begins for real.

7/15 Finished waterproofing the foundation walls on this very hot day, wedged in the cool space between raw earth & cement. Picked up our sills at the mill last night, & today the joists were delivered.

7/17 Stacked and stickered a major load of lumber today. The wood comes here in pieces, never to leave this spot.

7/18 The backfill. Cellar is finished.

7/20 Lesson in economics: worked and saved for five years, then passed it on to John in one huge check. He was worth it. David and Anne come tomorrow.

7/25 Started to build today, interrupted by a storm that knocked the corn down. First joist spans the concrete cellar, union of impermanent to permanent. Tomorrow we lay out the floor and climb slowly to the sky.

7/26 Anne serves us tea at 10 and 4, while David, Kal and I hammer hammer hammer. The garden gushes forth vegetables to feed the work. First wall of the house is framed and standing alone in the moonlight.

7/28 Just working, breaking, working, breaking—a symphony with pauses and rests. Evening is a blessing I am too tired to enjoy. Early morning is sweet and quickly spent.

8/1 First rafters up. Shape of our future appears against the sky.

8/5 Drinks in the new house—all framed—shouting happy and free in the garden.

8/8 August days are upon us, the walls are all closed in. David and Anne leave us here alone with the details. He wants nothing to do with an aluminum roof.

8/10 I drove off in the truck in the rain tonight till I was just far enough to be ready to come back, like the tide or a wave. No more than the usual up and down.

8/11 The house looms large. Finishing seems an impossible task. Spent time in the garden, renewing my love relationship w/ it.

8/12 First gallon of pickles this morning. Moved all the canned goods and canning supplies into the new cellar. Dreamt last night of the cellar filled w/ cabbage, brussels sprouts, apples.

8/13 The house stands roofless to the sky, and we survive w/ a sort of battered strength. Hammered nails in anger today for the first time, and they sure do go in fast that way.

8/16 Details hang from frayed ends, w/ no apparent progress on our roofless half-finished house.

8/17 Corn!

8/18 The roof, our greatest anxiety, goes halfway up, a long day in the sun. The view wonderful, the bodily movements strenuous, dangerous. We cover over our dwelling and make it a place of shelter, a home.

8/19 The roof. The sun. The stars.

8/20 Twice in the last two days we've been howling from the roof peak for failure and anguish and lack of a good reason why we are stuck with this experience which we've carved out for ourselves. How I hate the house for being there exactly as I plotted it on graph paper, only different in ways I could not foretell and wish were *not*.

8/21 The ridge cap is on, an unholy struggle.

8/22 Living here is a marriage, not a love affair—or so I feel tonight, having worked all day under a roof that really did keep out the rain. There was mud all around the house, up to my ankles in rubber boots, but tonight I can imagine a light on in there and somebody reading.

8/26 Still a long way to go—doors, stairs, window glass, insulation, woodstove & chimney, etc. Are the windows too narrow? Is the house too tall? I never would have recognized all this bulk and angularity as the cottage of my dreams.

8/29 I wanted to be far far away from The House, and not to think about it or see it anymore. But today we built one of the doors, and now I begin to imagine baking bread, sitting with my arms leaning on a table.

9/5 Labor Day, spent canning corn on the Coleman stove in the a.m. and wandering aimlessly but contentedly through the house. Now here I am, writing dutifully in my notebook. The "3 sentences" I've assigned myself feel like so many words. Serving my sentences.

9/8 Nothing. Nothing. Nothing.

9/10 Putting up fiberglass insulation makes a building feel more like a room. Coons got the corn.

9/12 Cold tonight. Frost? Big Dipper pours light all over our land.

9/15 The food is moving into the new house before we do! In the attic, herbs hang from the rafters, unshelled dry beans sit in bags on the floor. In the cellar, a row of this summer's jars, a box heaped w/ green & red peppers, 41 acorn squashes, potatoes, pickles.

9/16 It's hard to get up at 5:30 a.m. in the dark trailer. Coleman stove gives no comfort. But the more I do today, the sooner I will be able to wake in my own house and stoke up the cookstove for tea.

9/17 Scheduled events before we Move In: sheetrock on ceiling, boards on interior walls, doors hung, cookstove & composting toilet in working order, glass in the windows. A list makes it seem finite, but it sure ain't nothing.

9/25 Finished up the insulation and vapor barrier in the ceiling today. The "sheetrockers" come tomorrow. There's a big moon, & it's clear & cold—the first killing frost tonight?

9/27 The cookstove arrived today, & despite its 513 lbs., we handled it reasonably well. Rolled it across the plywood floor on iron pipes without even yelling at each other.

10/1 I feel so frustrated with these house-finishing details that I walk off into the woods, thinking if I go far enough I will disappear & not have to deal w/ my life any more. But it doesn't work that way.

10/3 By night I can believe in myself, by day I grow pessimistic. I fear coming through this experience w/ less, not more, self-respect than before. But I am still here, after five months, doing this work w/ unremitting attendance. That is something, I guess.

10/4 No chairs, no oven, no space, so it's pretty amazing that our daily life functions: even the yogurt culture we brought from New Hampshire is still alive. But meanwhile, I feel house-building as a blackness.

10/7 We moved in! I guess you could say it just happened. Cold cold night predicted. We raced all day. Kal connected the metal chimney sections up from the hole in the ceiling, through the attic, then walked up the slippery aluminum roof to make a hole to bring the chimney through. (Easier said than done.) I hung heavy blankets over the two doorways. Then errands in town, the afternoon getting colder and colder. When we got home to hook the stove to the chimney, we found we had the wrong size stovepipe. We screamed with rage and frustration. Too damn cold to stay in the trailer, but where else?, huddling in the dark, and suddenly out of nowhere Kal shouted, "Let's get the hell out of this fucking trailer." So we grabbed the mattress & sleeping bag & flashlights, & moved like thieves into our new house. Even w/o the stove in here, we were mighty comfortable.

10/8 Over the past few weeks we've been scurrying around, bringing in the squash, bringing in the onions, bringing in green tomatoes, bringing in red tomatoes—and finally, when the house was full, we brought in ourselves from out of the frosty night.

10/10 Spent the entire day painting the ceiling, a "canopy of peace" over us. The house looks wonderful at night, the one little lamp shedding light through all the windows of the one-room house.

10/13 Worked on the front door, canned 10 gallons of cider, helped Kal put composting toilet vent through the roof. Now that we've moved in, there's no transition from being "at home" in the trailer to "at work" in the house. We race towards evening rest, and then all energy turns toward arising when the alarm goes off at 6 a.m.

10/14 Discipline & perseverance. We put up the door today to hold out a predicted stormy gale. Let it rain.

10/16 I've been hard cider, fermenting, caught in the bottleneck. Hard cider, hard times. But today I feel uncorked, effervescent & free.

10/17 Each job brings an immediate change in our new life. Kal finished venting the toilet through the roof, & suddenly we abandon the beloved outhouse, and pee inside on a rainy night. We hung the other door, & suddenly it's quiet & secure in here. But I feel a pang: will I still hear the whip-poor-will when I'm living surrounded by the things of my life?

10/18 Today I nailed together & sanded the window frames. Not too long ago they didn't exist, except as boards, & longer ago, as trees. The very idea of a window is itself a newcomer to this place.

10/19 Compared to the land all around, this tiny protuberance of wood I call my home seems small. And yet it's my whole world. I run around like nobody's business but my own, wearing paths in the sod with my daily rounds.

10/20 The wind has changed from south to north. Night is deeper now, and so is wind and sleep and water in the well.

10/26 The man who delivered the glass today said doubtfully, "Are you going to see it through the winter?" Yes of course. "No electricity," he noticed, giving us an odd look. "It sure is quiet here," he finally confessed. "What are you going to do for food?" I pointed proudly toward the bulkhead, "Want to see the cellar?" We went down the dark steps. He looked appraisingly at the canned goods and full bushel baskets. "You folks have the right idea," he said with envious approval.

11/8 It is not always easy. It is not always hard.

Carrying Water as a Way of Life

1978

I carry water from a rock-walled spring to my house every day. This is not anything to brag about. It is simply a matter of fact.

The act carries me out my door and down across the grass, through the garden, and into a low secluded corner of my field. There, the men of this place two hundred years ago dug a wide hole ten feet deep, reaching down to a vein of water. They rocked up the hole with an intricate circle of stones, the wall fully four feet thick. Years let the grass grow back over most of it.

Then I came, and rearranged the jumbled top layer of large flat stones, ones you can stand or sit on to gaze into the water. I built a pole-and-bucket well sweep like the ancient Chinese. One spruce pole, with a bucket on the end, hangs down from another horizontal pole that pivots in a crotched cedar post. A heavy stone weights the far end of the horizontal pole, counterbalancing the full bucket as it comes up out of the spring.

Like the ancient Chinese, I live by the symbol of the well that never changes. Each day I lower the bucket into the water, feeling whatever I feel that day, seeing whatever I see. Water is the inner reality, and up it comes, pure and clear, no matter what the day may bring.

And what thoughts I have, down at the spring drawing water! I see my life, with all its past and future, compressed into the moment of hauling up the water that sustains me. Here I am, who studied in universities and lived in towns and cities, who visited museums and concert halls and discussed the existence of God; who struggled and breezed through thirty years, headed for this place, this day, this two-gallon bucket of water that will fill my cells and wash my face, that will carry me through to the next performance of this act.

The lowering and raising of the bucket centers me. All thoughts become purified in the clear stream of water as it swirls through the funnel into a jug. This is my existence. Here is where I am.

Not just the act of carrying water engages me, but the way of life that goes with that act. I am aware of water, of drops and dowsings. To live with a quantity of daily water that I am willing to carry, I must live simply. My meals can't be too complex, for the clean-up goes on in a small basin of water. All washings are recyclings. The water that rinses my hair can clean my feet. The water that moistens bean sprouts can wash my face. The water that scrubs potatoes can feed the house plants. Vegetable cooking water goes into the soup. Leftover herb tea gives me a refreshing mouthwash.

I love water. I savor the rich clear taste, rock and moss the delicate flavoring of my daily drink. I would no sooner throw out a half cup of clean water than I would discard the last of a fine old wine. The water is sacred to me. I am a vessel, preserving.

In winter there's more to it, this hauling of water. Bundled up, on snowshoes, I track my way across the blank field. The hypnosis of following my own path day after day opens me to a wide white

world of rabbit tracks and pine grosbeaks, wild etchings in the snow
and sky. Before big storms I stock up on water, then settle in and
let the good times roll. After the storm, I go into my comic routine,
the awkward act, on snowshoes, of shovelling out the counterweight
from under the snow so I can lower the boom. The bucket breaks
the thin layer of ice that forms overnight like a protective mem-
brane. Up comes ice water, and it is my ritual on such days to gaze
at the world through shards of the finest, clearest pane I ever saw.

Mishaps can happen, too, like falling over sideways on snowshoes into a deep drift, with two full jugs to tend to. Watch her
squirm! Or once, dropping the bucket into the spring, I got a chance
to practice my lifesaving skills by performing a quick rescue act
with a long stick. But mostly it is pleasant and serene to be a
woman living in this space age when all things are possible, living
for just a moment of every day as if none of the modern world had
ever happened.

My body becomes my pony, faithful little feet, strong limbs that
do the job day after day. I cease to be involved in it at all. I am the
motor behind the work, the woman carrying water. The water's
source is not me, but that hole in the ground where I am privileged
to share in streams running deep. I dip into earth's bounty. I lift
life to the surface, and I am washed clean.

Yes, it's inconvenient, in practical terms. How much easier it is
not to think about the water you use. To open the faucet and let
her run, this is a glory of another life. My life is small, the drops
are measurable, the thirst quenchable. And yes, I could wish that
the spring were up the hill from home, so that, like Jack and Jill, I
could come running down when the jugs were full. But the spring
is where it is, down in the vale, a stone-cool grove spiced with the
scent of fern and rock and water. I walk uphill to the house, steady,

my arms hanging straight from my shoulders as they are made to do, weighted by forty pounds of water.

It's the rhythm, the rhythm I dance to. Jugs and buckets and basins do their job. I am the carrier, the drinker, the washer. It is a choice. I could as easily turn on a faucet in a city apartment and let the water do the running. But here I am. This is my life, and it feels good to me.

Down to the Wire:
Life Without Electricity

1978

There's a slice in the woods. I call it my road, and when I came here it was a lane with grass growing down the middle of it. An unspoken code of ethics for drivers ruled who should back up the narrow road to the nearest turnaround and who had the right to go forward. I soon learned the code, and learned my neighbors' habits—Bob on his way to work, Lynne taking the boys to the school bus, Laura going to pick up the kids at nursery school, a truck full of raspberry pickers headed for the pond.

Then the phone poles came, straighter than oaks, stalking their way up the road, and men in yellow hardhats plying the ledgy ground with dynamite. They strung the wire that linked us to each other and to the world outside this road. Easy communication seemed a necessity, but we continued to enjoy life without electricity. We shared jokes with our neighbors about canning by flashlight, hauling water, cooling beer in a stream. Our lives were enriched by this common aberration.

But we were the newcomers. We had no children then. My neighbors, five years on the land, were tiring of their voluntary simplicity. They dreamed of television and running water, lights and power tools, blenders, ice cubes. What could I say to their assertion that I would feel the same when I had a child, when I had lived without convenience for all those years on the land?

So last year another two strands of wire were added to the poles. Men in yellow hardhats and silver face masks climbed the pole by my house in a chill December wind. Down the road, the lights went on; up the road the switchbox waited, ready for juice. I watched with apprehension, sensing imminent change. But I felt detachment, too, as I pictured those wires sagging with ice some freezing night, the power out. I would know nothing of such household calamities: the wire was passing right by my door, but it wasn't coming in.

We and our neighbors had discussed the power issue many times. Like swallows we would gather on the wire, chattering, balancing, then all fly off in our own direction. In the end, we stayed unplugged and they went ahead without us. Each to his own, the Yankee way.

Now I live within sight of a power line. The wire has become a tightrope for me. Not a temptation, but a baseline, a measuring device, a balancer. The simplicity of my life requires much complexity. The reward is in being here to deal with the complexity, not off in town earning money to pay for a false simplicity. For what is so simple about a nuclear power plant 30 miles downwind from here, an energy industry that grips this whole nation, hypnotized into wanting wanting wanting? It looks simple to turn on a faucet, switch on a light, put your peas in the freezer, but such simplicity scares me because I keep seeing behind it, the Wizard of

Oz a little old man at the controls, and maybe he's not such a nice little man either.

Naturally, people question my sanity. If it's insane to carry fresh cold water from a stone spring to my house each day, so be it. If it's insane to benefit from the light of day and rest when darkness comes, so be it. If it's somehow insane to share a single oil reading lamp with my husband as we sit quietly at the end of a day's work, then surely I must be crazy.

Indeed, there are other sides to this argument even for me. Like a tightrope walker, I am balanced yet I know I could fall. And what would falling off the rope be like? It wouldn't be so bad, I sometimes think. So I would hook up to Central Maine Power, and have some lights. I would pay my monthly bill somehow. I could stay simple.

But some nagging part of me cries out, preferring the quiet of a house that's not plugged in. No engines, no hum, no knocking in the night. Just owls and bullfrogs and wind in the trees. I like walking down into the cellar for a quart of milk, down into the cool dark earth. I like the different light that comes in on cloudy days and sunny days and blizzard days.

And I even like the coping. Each human endeavor becomes a challenge, something to figure out, analyze, solve. How do I keep clean, for example? In summer it's easy. A black plastic bag with a hose on it lies filled with water in the sun all day. After the work is done, and the sun comes golden through the poplars, we hang the warm bag on a tree and shower, free.

In winter? The current solution involves filling the same bag with water heated on the stove, hanging it from a beam and standing in a galvanized tub with a curtain around it. Nothing like stepping out of the shower and drying off while standing in front of the open oven of a wood cookstove!

And how do I preserve food? I can most of it on the woodstove, and use a solar dehydrator for peas and greens, herbs, fruits, eggplant and zucchini. I rely on the sometimes fickle sun to do this work for me, but once it's in the jar I have no worry about a power failure or a freezer breakdown.

And, oh, can it be funny to perch on that wire and watch myself do some of this coping, with good old Reddy Kilowatt pulsing his way right by my place. In view of this ready-made convenience, can you imagine lugging a 50-pound battery down the driveway and into the back seat of a Volkswagen once a week to charge up enough power while driving to switch on some lights at home? Or hooking up the woodstove to a small steam engine under the back porch, generating enough power to turn on the radio? Or investing in expensive solar cells to charge up the household battery? All these plans are under discussion here, while the current sails by not 100 feet from the house.

The possibility of hooking in saves me from far-fetched energy fantasies. What good are alternatives that modernize but don't relieve the complexities of simplicity? Until I can come up with plans that, from the ironic perspective of that wire, don't look harder than what I do now, I'll continue with this old-fashioned way of living.

After all, there were days when such easy power was not even available, and people managed to live rich, full lives nonetheless. Why should the fact that most people no longer saw lumber by hand, clean up with a broom, sew on a treadle machine, or grind flour in a hand mill keep me from enjoying the quiet industriousness of the old ways?

Living without electricity is a far cry from living an absolutely pure existence untainted by the evils of our world. Kerosene, for example, is this not a petroleum product? And flashlight batteries do not exactly grow on trees. We drive cars, go to the movies, and use the laundromat. There is no virtue in suffering, and if life without electricity should become a form of suffering, I would hook up as soon as possible.

But staying unhooked provides a philosophical tension wire that keeps me questioning, keeps me answering, keeps me questioning again. There are plenty of nights I am so tired that television sounds like a lot of fun, and I know I could have that too if I just plugged in. Then, quietly turning the page of my book, I say this is good too. Here is good. Stay here.

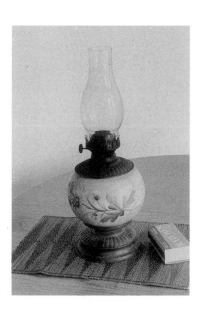

Jars

1978

My life is involved with jars. Up from the cellar I bring them, empty, to be filled. Down into the cellar I carry them, full. Up from the cellar I bring them, full, to be emptied. I clean them. I carry them down again. They feed me. I feed them.

Jars are transparent. Their being is nothingness, a vessel, a form to be filled with other forms, a colorless shape to contain colorful shapes. One year a jar is red with tomato sauce, the next year yellow with mustard pickle. Purple grape juice, amber apple sauce, pink rhubarb, green beans, brown chutney. From year to year the jar transforms. The same jar emits a different light.

Jars preserve a snapshot of the garden's beauty. Dill flowers and cucumber with floating garlic cloves. Corn and shell beans. Red peppers and green peppers. In jars we see reflected the delight of our summertime eyes, once winter comes and turns our brilliant patch of ground to limitless white.

Then there are the jars of grains, the muted browns and tans of rice and nuts and flour. Big gallon jars hold future breads and cereals, all their elements separated, waiting to be united by my hands. Dried foods, these too dwell in jars. Former juice jars and coffee jars and jelly jars of all sizes and shapes protect shrunken eggplant slices, curled apple rings, brittle spinach from the vapors of the air. There's cider, in gallon jugs that once held vinegar or juice. Dandelion wine, in old wine bottles gathered at parties. Home-brewed beer, in bottles worth more to me than their 5¢ deposit.

And of course, cartons and cartons of just jars, empty jars that might someday be useful for something. Jars seen at the dump, too good to pass up. Jars cleaned and saved from purchased mayonnaise, mustard, wheat germ. Jars that would look nice with flowers in them. Jars to put nails and screws in. Jars to keep garden seeds in. Jars to capture fireflies in. Jars for honey. Jars to catch the drip from a leaking roof. Jars to give as gifts, filled with herb teas or dried fruit or maple syrup.

And doesn't every woman keep a mental list of who has a jar of hers, whose jar she has? Homestead ecology requires a balance of jars. In them we gather all that we sow. In them we preserve the fruits of our labor. They contain our continuing life.

Passing them through my hands time and time again, I become one with jars. I too am a vessel, a temporary dwelling for the stuff of life. I too am a transparent space existing in the midst of time. My life too is a series of transformations. What is it that fills me, empties me, changes my light? I reflect the universe as it flows through me. I am intimately involved with jars.

The Old Well

1982

Standing at the bottom of the second well we found on our place, I am sixteen feet under. Deeper than dead, and as cold. Surrounded by a cylinder of stone, I look up at a circle of sky the size of an eye. I see, just barely, Kal's face peering down. I feel above-ground life over me, the top of sod, the bushes and trees growing out of sod like the earth's hair. I am under, separated from root-hairs in a cylinder of stone.

There's no water in here now. I stand with high boots on the cold clay, a softness that does not give way to sinking. The clang of buckets bumping against the sides has ceased, the last broken bottle removed, the last flat fallen rock tied with rope and hauled up, the last of the soft sinking mud scooped out. Now I am alone in the cold cylinder.

I should be jubilant. I have restored what was ruined, made good this well they dug and built two hundred years ago. I have made restitution to the appetites of uncaring time. I have done homage to human labor, ambition, necessity.

But I am not jubilant. I am defeated. I am chilled. I may even be dead, dropped down the cold stone cylinder, dropped down sixteen feet and down two hundred years into the dry well. Here I await the coursing of water through subterranean veins, the filling up, the hauling out of bucket after bucket of life-sustaining fluid. But now, down in the cold dry well, I am dead.

Unless I bend my neck back very far, craning until my hardhat bumps the rocks behind me in this narrow space, to view the blue circle of light and life above me, unless I arch myself into this unnatural position, all I see is darkness, grey rocks mottled with lichen, brown mud. Unless I strain myself toward light and life, scrambling up the rocks for one last time, finding footholds in the crevices of the past, then I am dead, then I will die, and coil myself like a snake at the bottom of this old well, waiting for water to fill my grave.

I should be jubilant after four days of backbreaking labor, climbing down first just eight feet to where the rubble begins, jiggling loose a fallen rock, tying the rope around it, climbing out, hauling it up. Then down again, spying water between the rocks. This must be the bottom; ten feet should be deep enough for one of these old shallow wells.

But ten feet turns to twelve, thirteen, fourteen, as rocks removed reveal more fallen rocks. My fingers, arms, legs, back begin to break, my spirit breaks. Memory of those who dug this well so long ago no longer sustains my labor. But down I go again, tying, climbing out, hauling up. Each round gets harder, farther from the light. I lose my certainty that there will be a hard solid bottom where I can retrieve the prize, two dozen bucketsful of broken glass, rusty metal, rotten boards, and mud.

In the end I stand in the hole sixteen feet under, looking up at a distant sky. They say you can see the stars at midday from the bottom of a well, but I must not be deep enough for that. I see blue, the blue sky that lifts our spirits when we're on the ground. But I am not on the ground, to be lifted up in joy. I am under ground, deeper than dead, the blue disk above me a timeless illusion of light and life.

I could stand here now forever, in the silence of no more clanging buckets. I know I must climb out before the veins begin to swell with water, the tourniquet of choking years released. But I am chilled to inertia at the bottom of the cylinder. I am lost, travelling down through space and time into the heart of old man Sukeforth who dug this well with his boys while the women and girls rolled out biscuits and kept the garden hoed. I am the dead old man who dug this well to give his family life.

Fire finally wiped out all they had made here. Not all, of course. The land remains, and lilacs blooming every spring by the fallen cellar. The whip-poor-will calls as usual, but no young child falling asleep under a quilt sewn of old shirt scraps can hear it. Grouse now live in the old cellarhole, nestling under the fallen leaves, oblivious to broken crockery and the rusted old stove.

One morning she was frying donuts, they say, sending them out to the men plowing the field. Suddenly, flames leap out of the skillet, flames hotter than fresh fried donuts. Oil come alive jumps to the pine plank floor. Children! she cries, children, run to the well. Run to the field. Run to the neighbors.

Grabbing the baby she flees her home before the flaming oil engulfs her kitchen, eating the long trestle table worn with meals, the rocking chairs, the beds. Flames lick the windows clean, flames tumble down the front steps.

The men arrive breathless from the field. The flames consume their home as lightly as hungry men downing donuts. Buckets of water drawn from the well are of no use, mere thimbles. Helpless, they set down their buckets and watch the timbers cave in, the floor crack, the stove crash through into the cellar, the crocks of salted-down cabbage burst, the bushels of potatoes char. The flames, running out of food, subside and die, leaving ashes by the lilac bush, leaving nothing but the well.

Old man Sukeforth can't weep in his wife's arms. He must be the strong arms, hitching the horses, loading the wagon with children, looking back one last time at the blackened remains of all his work. No tears. Maybe even anger, as he pitches a bottle down the well, farewell, what the hell, no one will drink from that circle of water again.

Now I stand down here at the bottom of his labors, deeper than dead, further under than he is buried now, far below the groping lilac roots, darker than dust. I found the old man's broken bottle, broken well-cover, broken pole and bucket, broken dreams. I revived them all, brought them up into light and life. Now I must bring up myself, making myself climb up and up the carefully laid stone circles, making myself return to the temporality of above-ground life. My house could fall down too, will fall down no matter what I do, and who will restore it? Some young dreamer a hundred years from now, admiring my overgrown asparagus bed, lying in the shade of the maples I planted, eating my apples. There is no permanence in nature, but cycles of work and destruction and revival.

I climb up, stone after stone, feeling history in my aching bones, one volume closed and another begun.

Power of Choice: The Sun

1983

By five years, we'd succeeded in our goal. A small, passive solar house kept us warm on one cord of wood. A large garden and root cellar kept us well fed. We carried water, lit with kerosene, and cooked with wood. We even had the luxury of an indoor composting toilet. But simplicity is complex. While I never believed that the simple life meant the easy life, what I didn't foresee was the strenuous personal quest that lay before us as we grew with these choices.

Alternative lifestyles provoke controversy. Even more than the lack of a flush toilet, living without electricity made us an object of curiosity. We had taken a stand, and, like it or not, we were often called upon to answer for it. In my case especially, the stand had a way of solidifying, for in my work as a writer I extolled this chosen life. But all my essays and poems about the simple life made me want to spend more time writing and less on "grunt labor." Now I faced the hidden challenge: how to alter my position without destroying what I value.

It was hard to admit to conventional desires. Wouldn't I love to hear the sound of ice cubes tinkling in a glass once again, or the click of an electric switch flooding my house with light? But, once confessed, the harder part was trying to mesh these desires with the unconventional principles that still held true. That pulsing power line 100 feet from our door offered us a fast conversion. We could ease up on all this labor with a freezer, a refrigerator, lights, water pump, and so on. We just had to call the power company and sign our name. And pay the bills, of course. But kerosene wasn't all that cheap anymore either, and the fumes in our tightly constructed house worried us. Hooking up to the grid would clearly be the easiest solution.

But easy scared me after so much hard. I saw how suddenly I might find myself living someone else's life, driving off to work each morning so I could pay the bills instead of walking down to the spring for my daily water. Five years of hauling water seemed long, but how would thirty years of "working out" be?

Then we learned that people right here in Maine were installing photovoltaics, or solar electric power. Though highly technological, photovoltaics make harmonious use of an infinite resource, the sun. Photovoltaics are costly and provide only limited power (no refrigeration, for example, without many "panels"), but they fit our desire to alter, not destroy, our small-scale, self-reliant life. We clearly wanted to electrify our life, and now it was a question of how: with cheaper unlimited "grid" power, or with costly limited photovoltaics?

Most residential photovoltaic system owners do not live within sight of a public power line, as we do. Up on a mountain or out on an island, one can reasonably expect to find solar "arrays" where gasoline generators are the only alternative. But, seeing that power line out of the corner of our eye, we were obviously not concerned with what was reasonable. From an economic point of view, central power would clearly cost us less. But everyone knows that power rates rise as fossil fuels diminish, and nuclear power is not exactly free. And what will nuclear waste disposal or possible contamination cost? Photovoltaics would cleanly and quietly produce electricity for life. Surely we could afford to pay for that peace of mind.

Such economic reasoning brought us finally to this paradox: cheaper central power might end up costing more; costly photovoltaics might well be a bargain.

We came so close to choosing public power that we went down to Sears to price freezers, and then paid a visit to the Central Maine Power office. Get the house wired, said the representative, and call us for the "power drop." We left the office in a daze, inexorably moving toward what we suspected we didn't really want. We found ourselves haunted by nostalgic regret. The quiet of the house and woods and garden kept whispering, Please, reconsider.

I saw that coming here had been a conscious choice. I had believed that living and writing about this life would be my contribution to change in the world. Did I value my principles so little that for cheap convenience I would turn my back on my beliefs? How could I write about change while my electric typewriter hummed with splitting atoms? But I also saw how hard I had tried to be consistent without ever questioning "consistency." Was it possible, or even desirable, that my actions never contradict my beliefs?

We did finally choose the hard way—photovoltaics—but we did not kid ourselves that it was morally consistent. That desire went out with the kerosene lamps and water jugs. We ended up with photovoltaics because we continued to value the pioneering spirit that brought us to the puckerbrush in the first place. Years of gardening had taught me that change is in the nature of things, yet I'd been resisting change in my own life, doggedly limiting myself to a worn-out definition of who I thought I was. "Getting power" gave me power, the power to accept my own changes along with those in the woods and fields around me.

I'm not living someone else's life now, any more than I was before. It's still my own life, even as I flick the switch. We live by power generated from our own choices, a personal resource that never runs out, and from the sun which lasts longer even than that.

Beans Are Us

1988

We were kneeling on the plywood subfloor, Chris and I, unrolling the pink fiberglass and cutting it to length, when we got to talking, as we did every morning since the day he showed up in his battered truck ready to cut a hole through the east wall of our house and add on ONE LAST TIME, I swear it, a dining room this time, with a pretty window and a glass door. I'd already told him the whole story of how Kal and I had remodeled twice before in the fourteen years since we built our passive solar house. The first time was less than a year after we'd "finished," though I say "finished" advisedly, since what owner-built home ever is? It was a one-room house, for the first winter anyway, was what I told Chris.

He just chuckled as he deftly changed the blade of his Exacto knife and stood up to stuff a stud-space with insulation. He lived in a one-room house himself and knew all about "homesteading," being a retired *Mother Earth News* reader like ourselves. He could surely appreciate our practical notion of living in one room and storing everything that wasn't absolutely necessary for daily life in the other room, which was an unfinished attic accessible by ladder.

But he wasn't the least bit surprised when I told him how, the very next summer, we cut through our brand-new joists to make a stairway to the attic, which we insulated and sheetrocked and called by the name of bedroom. That's where we all slept, by then there was a baby too, and we called the downstairs by the name of living-dining-cooking room, all serviced by one Aladdin kerosene lamp and a wood cookstove. Simple, yes; practical, yes; cramped ... yes. Chris unrolled another bundle of pink glass, and nodded sympathetically.

That's when I decided to change the blade in my knife, too, so I could cut that fiberglass with one good stroke and get on with it. The story, that is, which seemed to go with the job as peanut butter goes with jelly. You should always tell your carpenter everything, so he'll know if you're the kind who'll want the plywood subfloor nailed down good and tight with annular nails every 2 inches, or if every 6 will do. That can make a difference in materials and labor, but using the maximum of nails can save you some big trouble down the line, with squeaks and so forth. Chris had no doubt already deduced that I wasn't the type who'd want any squeaks, and he encouraged me to tell him the rest of the story, in case he'd missed any important implications from the first part. Besides, we'd had a lot of coffee, and he, an aging hippie like me, was finding the whole thing rather amusing, a typical homesteader's history was what he called it. I imagine he'd heard a lot of them before in his remodeling career, from the way he kept smiling knowingly as I rattled off the details. The real truth is, and we both knew it, it's hard to live by your own principles because of a little thing called change. Even principles can change, just the way those stone walls that line all the overgrown fields can topple with the passing of time. In fact, I've learned the sad truth that even the nature of change itself can change, making it all the harder to live an honest life. But I'm not going to let the march of human foolishness get me down, even if it takes cutting my own fiberglass of an August morning.

Anyway, I told Chris that about three years after the stairway project I'd returned to college teaching, from which I'd been a dropout very early on. I was the one among my college friends who didn't drop out in the 'sixties when it was fashionable. I hate doing things when they're fashionable. You might have already suspected that, since here I am still homesteading well into the 'nineties when I'm supposed to be microwaving myself into corporate heaven. But me, I did my climbing in the 'sixties, just kept on getting degrees until I finally reached "the terminal degree" and had to go out and earn a living, another unfashionable pastime of those days. I lucked out, though, because the college where I landed my first job in 1972 went bankrupt two years later, and by then I'd discovered there was a whole world out there beyond the ivy walls, a whole world of trees to sit under and gardens to hoe, and that's when I married the former dean of students and entered the homesteading business. (Meanwhile my hippie college friends were on their way back to law school. I just waved at them from under the apple tree. They left all their long skirts to me, and of course I had my own perfectly good new pair of bare feet.)

Once we'd made the break from one-room to two-room living (typical career pattern of the 'seventies homesteader, said Chris), I had to leave off hoeing and go back to teaching part-time. The big difference was the way I played it this time, as the mad professor with the double life, reading student papers by kerosene light and hauling five gallons of water each morning before starting out on the hour commute to the college. On Sunday nights, I had to scrub my nails and knees after a weekend in the garden. Soon after that we hired a crew to help us build a two-story addition bigger than the original house, with a room for our son, a study for me, and a living room. And of course we had to get electricity to run the new . . . Chris had already guessed it . . . television. "Solar electricity, though," he added to mollify me. Yes, I said, don't think I was a complete sell-out. I lucked out again, because the dean I married turned out to be a hard-core alternative lifestyle freak, committed to composting everything, including human waste. I'm proud to say it's our system of dealing with the waste stream that continues to exclude us from the mainstream, and I owe it all to Kal. Alone, I could have mustered the strength to grow zucchini, but together we took on the whole of American cultural values, and we were committed body and soul. And checkbook. It costs a lot to "live free or die."

I could tell by a certain hunch in Chris' fiberglass-fuzzed shoulders that this story was getting to be too much for him. He already knew perfectly well that when you build a house, you dig a hole in the ground and pour all your money into it, and the bigger the hole, the more it takes to fill it. He was still in the one-room phase, and maybe he was sensitive about it. He was a college graduate, too, and an avid reader. No television for him. This guy had more ideas than all of my professional colleagues put together. Maybe I'd just shut up for a while, now that he'd heard nearly the whole story, or enough to know what kind of woman he had here on his crew. A woman who abandoned first a full-time career as a professor, and then a career growing zucchini, in order to learn the art of carpentry first-hand because of some damn-fool notions about the way life should be. Notions, I might add, that he shared. There are still some "'sixties throw-backs" out here in the boonies. We were about done with the fiberglass, anyway, and I needed a break.

I stood with my arms outstretched on the rough opening in the wall that would be the windowsill, surveying through the flapping plastic what would be the view from the new dining room. I have a way of looking at views like this, wherein I've learned to levitate piles of rocks into beautifully terraced gardens all planted in peonies and delphiniums, and under the old lilac instead of seeing a heap of bent nails, tar paper, roof shingles, and lumber scraps, there I envision a little white table with me sitting and sipping my coffee, relaxed and cool as can be. This type of vision takes practice, but I've had a lot of it in the years of stamping out milkweed in favor of lawn. This very spot where I was standing, leaning on a soon-to-be windowsill, was once nothing but a caved-in cellarhole with cedar trees growing up out of it and a nesting pheasant. I remember the day Kal and I finally closed on the land and began our homesteading saga, before we'd even discovered the whole string of beaver dams in "our" backwoods, before we'd broken any ground for a garden, before we'd moved our funky pink trailer onto the place, before the dirt road was widened and phone poles brought in, we were sitting up there on the broken stone wall imagining the woman who once planted this lilac bush, those orange lilies, outside her kitchen door. We wanted to look out on her flowers, that was the kind of continuity we sought in coming to this scruffy little town that wasn't even on the map, to this narrow road that was really a trail through hundreds of acres of unclaimed woodland, and now with this new window at last we would share her vision of the world.

Of course her vision of the world was limited, and that's what we liked about it, having seen enough of the modern world not to want it. She planted her lilies, she raised her children and her garden, and she probably went to Rockland once or twice in her whole life, if that. In those days, people did for themselves, and traded at the many stores our little town had back then, dry goods and blacksmiths and coopersmiths, and they hauled oak logs, using horses, to the stave mills along the river. Church and Grange, one-room schoolhouse, graveyards. Every one of the caved-in cellars marked with an old lilac bush that line these dirt roads was a farm, back then. I suppose Rockland, twenty miles away on the coast, seemed as distant to the lady of the lilies as Boston or New York seem to me now. What I wanted was to create something with my labor, something to leave as a legacy, like her lilies and lilacs. I wanted to live on the land, with the land, to build shelter and grow food and find my place in the natural order. And I have succeeded in all that, I'm proud to say. But a dining room with a glass door? Is that to be my legacy, if by chance it were left standing a century from now?

"Let's get started on this vapor barrier," I hear Chris say, calling me back from my wistful windowsill. Vapor barrier? I think, what for? Dining room, what for? I can eat beans anywhere. Just give me a wooden bowl and a plank to set it on. I turn from the would-be window and cast a sad, though satisfied, eye on the silver-foil walls. Chris knows this look. He knows the bewildered, ambivalent look of an honest person swept along by an eddy of change. It's all in a day's work, for him.

"You deserve it," he says. "Here, let's unroll this stuff."

We both kneel worshipfully on the subfloor again, which is where Kal finds us when he drives up with a load of sheetrock. No rough-pine wallboards this time, in this one last addition. This one's going to bring us right up to the present day, right smack into the building boom that's threatening to turn our rural county into suburbs, of what urb don't ask me. We were the two who balked at the advice to paint, stain, or otherwise chemically protect our windowframes. What? we gasped. Use something not found in nature? Either that, or let 'em rot, said David, our carpenter-advisor back in 1977, and so our trim became blue and so did we. Now here comes this load of sheetrock, this tub of joint compound, these cans of latex.

I'm just getting up from the floor to help unload the truck when I hear a vehicle coming up the road. Ever since Kal and I came here, the sound of a vehicle coming up the road has been a call to action, tantamount to someone saying "Let us rise for the national anthem." We stop whatever we're doing, and rush to the front window. Until we added this one last addition, though, it was a futile effort to see the road from the front windows through lilacs. Now, the pretty new window faces the road directly, with only the tall pine trunks as a barrier. I squint through the plastic, and even thus distorted, the shape of the shiny new Jeep is clearly that of the local realtor. I can't imagine why anyone would want a white Jeep. For driving through white mud, perhaps? He went by yesterday, too, and I thought nothing of it, but as I wait by the window for him to come back down again—another verse in our anthem tradition—suddenly I notice strips of blaze-orange surveyor's tape flapping in the wind on some innocent trees across the road.

My heart lurches in my chest, and I drop my Exacto knife. My hands are shaking as I jump down from the opening where the glass door will go, and I run down the driveway roaring like a lion. Chris and Kal, sliding sheetrock out of the truck, flash frightened looks in my direction. They know what I'm like when I have to unload materials this close to lunch. But I usually don't run away, so they become alarmed by my outbreak and follow me into the road. I'm still roaring as I watch Kal's mouth drop open, and he grabs his hair, a gesture of anxiety I've seen when, for example, he's just climbed all the way up the slippery aluminum roof to clean the chimney only to find he forgot his rope. Chris hitches up his nail belt and takes off his hat like a man at a funeral.

Orange tapes can mean only one thing, and we all know it: the hundred acres of woodland across the road are no longer "unclaimed." The rugged forest with its many boulders, its fallen trunks and acres of rotting leaves, its dead and down, its live and well, its swampland and hillocks, is all of a sudden, through no fault of its own, a commodity in a soaring market where land can change hands two or three times within a year, the price doubling each time. Speculators who never set foot on the land, who might view the road frontage through the windshield of a white Jeep, or maybe only take a look at the survey map in the real estate office, will pass the title that's been in one family for two hundred years as easily as someone at a Bean Supper passes the macaroni down the table to the next hungry guy.

But their profit will be our loss. If I could believe that people would buy land here for love, not money, that they would put down roots and stay for life, all right, times change. But I've seen enough forests felled and stone walls hauled off to be sold in town, I've seen the price of land rise so high that no mere family can buy it, but only a developer, a banker, a speculator, a businessman. I've seen what becomes of the earth when everything is taken from it in exchange for money. The Jeep goes by, a passenger in a pin-striped suit looks out at us and the realtor waves, kind of friendly-like, at three dumbfounded old hippies standing by the side of the dusty road. I've stopped my roaring, for now, and we all go back up to unload the sheetrock and eat our baked bean sandwiches.

For Love or Money

1988

No doubt about it, I'd be charitable to call our fly-ridden jungle a paradise, but give it the best efforts of your youth and I suppose you could call it a diamond in the rough. When we moved "way back in," naturally our family and friends thought we had gone completely mad, but it really did surprise me that even the towns-people here raised their eyebrows when we told them "where'bouts" we'd settled.

"Isn't that the old Sukeforth place?" they would ask. "Ayuh, I ain't been up there for years. That road's pretty well growed in by now, ain't it? Used ta be an old horse-n-buggy path, back when I was small. Couldn't get through with a Jeep last time I tried."

I can still remember our first public appearance in town after we moved in. It was May, and you don't have to be born in Maine to know what that means. Black flies. We moved here from New Hampshire, so we were well acquainted with the darling critters already, but now we were living surrounded by hundreds of acres of woods, and without a screen porch for retreat. The pink trailer we'd moved to our land for shelter while we built the house was hot as an oven in the day, so we figured we'd just keep on working to clear the house site and start the garden, and save resting for the cool evenings. That meant an all-day feed for the black flies, and they just love new blood, even if it's only imported from right across the border. Natives, if you've noticed, don't seem to be bothered by the bugs. One test of your birthright is can you wear a halo of flies without suffering a single bite. I sure flunked that test, and I can still remember the glances I got from the locals, a cross between sympathy and amusement, when we showed up at our first Grange supper one Saturday night. Lost for a week in the Allagash, that's how I looked, face all covered with red welts, especially along my hairline and behind my ears, eyes all swollen. That didn't stop me from eating my gallon of beans, though, and a few slices of pie to wash it down. And then it was back up the ridge to haul brush out of the old cellarhole and feed the bugs. If only we could have harnessed those flies, we'd have been done a lot sooner. As it was, we relied on bow-saws, clippers, and a Gardenway cart, and it took from May till July to get the site ready for excavation and building.

Black flies aren't all, though. Then come the mosquitoes, followed by the deer flies, and during really humid weather, the grand slam, all three at once. Or should I say the grand slap. When John drove up hauling a bulldozer, ready to scoop out our cellar, he just about jumped right back into the cab of his dump truck after five minutes' jawing with us in the driveway. "You guys got to be nuts," he jibed, pointing through the glass of his closed window at my bleeding face and neck. "You ain't gonna last." But last we did. And the bugs have lasted just as well, nicely fed on the blood of imported organic gardeners.

Now don't get me wrong, I'm not complaining. Not about the flies, anyway. If I didn't like it here I'd have moved long ago to Portland, Boston, San Francisco, or at least to Camden, like so

many of our back-to-the-land generation. The reason I'm telling
you all this is that, would you believe it, this ledgy ridge of un-
tamed, fly-infested woods that was originally given as payment (or
maybe punishment) to Hessian mercenaries who fought for the
British in the Revolutionary War, and that ten-fifteen years ago
could be had for a song, will cost you a grand opera today. Yes sir,
I mean to tell you they're logging off the ridge. Top-heavy trucks
careen over the bumps and ruts of our one-lane road at breakneck
speed, carrying their cargo of big pines and oaks to the mill. Empty
bottles and cigarette packs, oil cans, greasy rags litter the side of
the road. But, get ready, worse is yet to come: now that the woods
have been "cut off," the land is up for sale again. And here's where
the story gets really contemporary.

We bought our land cheap in 1977 because it was "cut-over
woods." As I said, a diamond in the rough. Very rough. The woods
were dense with slash piles and raspberry thickets, rotting stumps
of spruce and pine and oak, the woods-road gouged with deep ruts.
What I liked about it was the huge lichen-covered boulder that no
bulldozer could ever hope to move, the old stone bridge that crossed
a usually-dry stream, and the vision of what the woods could be if
we cleaned them up. Which we haven't, but never mind that. And
I admit, I do like the second-growth poplar that some call useless,
the way the leaves whisper in the wind. And I like the quiet of no
more chainsaws, the feeling that I own a hunk of land that has
been stripped of any value except to me and the wildlife.

But this newly logged land up the road, denuded of its beauty,
studded with boulders and rough hills and vales, isn't going for the
bargain price of "cut-over woods," which used to be realtor talk for
"it's a mess, you young fools, take it if you want it, and good luck to
ya" back in the 'seventies. Realtors have a different way of talking
in the 'eighties, something along the lines of "views possible." The

acreage, which as far as I can tell has views that would make anyone but a bulldozer cry, has been cut into two parcels, each going for twice the price of the original piece. Do you follow me? That's a mark-up four times the initial investment, plus the profits from lumber sales.

The way I figure it, there's nothing to keep me here now except an acquired taste for deer flies in my hair, black flies in my eyes, and mosquitoes in my ears. That, and a decade's investment of backbreaking labor, and a pretty decent garden after all, and no place I'd rather be. In an effort to preserve these simple pleasures, I've been thinking about erecting a roadside stand at the base of my driveway. "FREE ADVICE." I'd stop those potential buyers and tell them how the road gets so narrow in winter, with snowbanks piled on the sides, that one car can scarcely fit through, and if you meet another car coming at you, a quick game of chicken determines which of you will back up the icy, curvy mile to the nearest turnout. I'd tell them that actually winter is nothing, it's spring you have to worry about, when those same snowbanks melt into the concave road creating one hell of a mess. I'd tell them that no schoolbus or mail car will call here unless the road is widened, but that the town voted years ago to leave these back roads as they are. And I'd tell them about the three or four days a year, sometime around Halloween, when you can sit outside bug-free enjoying your "possible views" before deer-hunting season begins and you have to take cover. Although I suppose, with the woods cut off, the deer won't be around to be hunted much longer. There's some good in every bad. And as you can see, I'm trying hard to find it.

Of course, I'm experienced at seeing the good in the bad. You don't spend years laboring to make a home in the middle of the woods without learning that. Now, surveying my green lawn, lush vegetable garden, young orchard, garden shed, neat house com-

plete with hollyhocks and rebuilt stone walls, I could easily forget
the view we had the day we straddled the rafters to put the metal
roofing on, and found, to our dismay, that each panel had gone on
just a little bit out of square so that when we got to the last piece it
jutted unevenly over the eaves, and it was dusk and starting to
rain and the mosquitoes were eating us alive and we were hungry
and frustrated, and my husband was shaking his fist at the sky
and yelling, "I'm not such a bad guy! I don't deserve this!" Looking
down from the dangerously slippery aluminum heights of our cre-
ation, we beheld a panorama of rock piles and subsoil, lumber scraps
and witchgrass, and the old pink trailer engulfed in milkweed. But
we're here now, aren't we? So it can't be all bad.

This tale of modern economics really began about five years
back when all us penniless homesteaders discovered that our work
had produced something worth money after all. Believe it or not,
there are folks out there who would pay good city-earned cash to
buy what we've created out of love or insanity. So what's to stop us
from throwing in the grimy old towel and buying a nice thick one?
Life in the boonies can wear pretty thin, I admit, especially once
you start commuting to town to earn a living. We all came here
filled with the dream of growing an acre of strawberries to cover
our taxes and vehicle expenses, and that's all the money we'd ever
need. We'd grow our own food, have potluck suppers with our
friends, and drive the old Volkswagen forever. But tell me what
happens when the old Volks finally drops its rusted-out floor dragging bottom on the muddy road one March day on the way to Town
Meeting, and a new car, even a new used one, costs twice your
annual income? What happens when the clothes you brought with
you when you made the Big Move are all patch-on-patch, and your
taxes are going up 20% a year but your income from selling camomile blossoms isn't? And what happens when the kid is born, not

talking goats here, a real live human baby who shortly grows up with needs and desires of his own? Now you're getting into the big bucks, not talking male deer here, and one fine day your friendly neighborhood realtor will come panting up your driveway, swatting at flies with a rolled-up survey map, to help you out of your fix.

Times they are a-changin', we sang way back in hippier days, and we're a-changin' along with them, just not quite as fast. Driving along in the slow lane, or maybe it's the breakdown lane, we're evolving slowly, by natural selection. Survival of the craziest. Once we were the "newcomers," and by now, at least on this road, we're getting to be the "old-timers." But don't fool yourself, it's all relative. You can't confuse "old-timer" with "native." That you can never be, nor your children either, even if they were born here. As the locals say, "If the cat has kittens in the oven we don't call 'em biscuits."

Still, we've earned a place here, at least as far as the deer and woodchucks are concerned. They never had it so good: kale and green beans, boy, these new folks sure can put on a good feed! And I like to think the trees need me, and even the grouse and whippoor-wills who lived in the overgrown cellarhole before we came have adjusted to the new tenants. I guess life here has made me just ornery enough to tell that realtor a thing or two when he makes me an offer I can resist. I mean, how could I ever trust anyone else to keep the weeds out of the asparagus patch, or prune the apple trees just so? For all I know, this place could go to someone who would just let the porcupines take over, and that really makes me bristle. No, it's for love, not money, that I stay here feeding the flies. There's nothing I can do to change the way things are going out there, but who says I have to go that way too? Looks like I'll be here until the cows come home, and since I don't even keep cows I guess that'll be quite a spell.

Sign of the Times: FOR SALE

1989

The thing about developers is, there's no way they're ever going to *live* on the good earth they're buying up around the State o' Maine. If you think for a minute that our pin-striped friend knows what he's buying, you're about as naive as a nudist in a north country spring. The realtor, maybe. After all, he wears plaid shirts and boots from L. L. Bean. But even that famous Maine outfitter has gone upscale, with a fake trout pond in the middle of its brand-new pine-panelled store in Freeport. Everything, even the venerable Bean's, changes when you add money to it. Except, I'm happy to say, the yellow-eye beans our local Grange serves up one Saturday night a month. Baked beans made this town great, and the trail of cars that line the road on those Saturdays attests to the enduring power of rural values. Let's face it, land is valuable for the beans it grows. Once you adopt the view that land is a commodity, you're well on the way to mass starvation. So it's with a humanitarian purpose that I will exert my professorial influence in this town by proposing a solution to the problem of land speculation. I say, if they want to buy land, let 'em live on it.

48

This may seem like an impractical proposal, but I can't help it, I'm still a professor. Drawing upon my knowledge of world literature, I invoke Tolstoy's question: how much land does a man need? If he is correct in asserting that all a man needs, in the end, is a plot about 4 feet by 7 feet, the problem of land speculation ends right there. But in this country of free enterprise, nothing should stand between a person and an idea on how to get ahead, not even death. Before you get the wrong idea, though, understand that I'm not saying we should put developers to death, as in the bumper sticker "Keep Maine Green: Shoot a Developer." No. What I'm saying is we should put developers to work. If they want to talk development, fine by me. If they want to talk growing food and planting trees and protecting wildlife habitats, if they want to talk affordable housing and energy-efficient buildings, if they want to talk community effort and local pride, okay, let's talk. There's more than one way to draw a bottom line.

Before I go on, I should warn you that I am subject to bouts of madness brought on by blackfly and mosquito season, which coincides with the most active period in the local real estate market. As the town's millions of trees begin to leaf out each May, you'd swear there is a new species of tree that bears blaze-orange leaves and grows primarily along road frontage or at a corner where stone walls meet. In the fall when the market slows down, these leaves, which are really surveyors' ribbons, blend in with the brilliant foliage and can be mistaken for orange-garbed hunters stalking deer. The man hired to survey our neighboring forest this fall, armed only with a transit and tape measure, confessed his terror at being in the woods with hunters hiding behind every hemlock. These woods offer the interloper his choice of ordeal, depending on the season: he can be the target of trigger-happy humans or blood-thirsty bugs.

If it were me, I'd choose the bugs. Somehow the maddening experience of being sucked by thousands of uncontrollable creatures, each smaller than a carrot seed, brings a person down to a more honest level of existence. It makes us realize our place in the food chain. It's encouraging to think that we have a necessary place in the lives of these creatures, instead of the usual bad rap about how we're destroying the planet. It's nice to feel needed. So what if the bugs drive us out of our mind? It's worth it, just to feel loved. Besides, some of my most viable ideas arise from bug-mania, such as this, my revised definition of "native": *any person, wherever their place of birth, who has lived in Maine for a minimum of fourteen years and whose blood tests positive for blackfly Serum B, which makes the subject immune to certain rational arguments.*

Being a professor, I am fortunate that my madness waits for the month of May after the semester's over. Summer marks the time for me to obey the prime mandate of my profession: to entertain the implications of my ideas, mad or not. My observations have led me to wonder if "true" natives, those actually born in Maine and bug-injected every year of their life, would consistently test positive for Serum B. Further research into the matter shows that, in fact, these native-born natives soon become immune to their own antibodies. This finding has one unfortunate consequence: native-born natives lose their ability to resist "certain arguments" in favor of the development of Maine land. And since they're the ones that own the land now eagerly sought by developers, this immunity threatens grave changes in the state land-use patterns.

I'm aware that it's easy for me to support resistance to development. I live on the land, as many "true" natives have for generations, and I owe them allegiance for teaching me to use my hands, my back, and my wits in ways that academia never did. And yet the truth is, I may bake my own bread but I don't earn my bread on the land. I did have dreams of raising camomile blossoms as a cash crop, but those were the halcyon days when I was young and barefoot. You need money, and that's got to be the hardest fact of life. So you sell what you have to sell in order to get what you need. If you have literary talent, you sell that. If you have land, you sell that. I would still argue, though, that land, not money, sustains our life. You can't eat money. Remember that.

Too bad there's never been a generation of born-and-bred natives that could make money on the land, unless they sold it. If your blood runs rich with blackfly serum you might say, in a moment of beneficial madness, that at least you do have the land. And what you probably mean by "you have the land" is: you have something of value, something capable of sustaining life, something to pass on to your children. If, on the other hand, you lack the important antibody, or if its effect has worn off because you were born in Maine and never saw New Jersey, "you have the land" might mean something else: you have something worth money.

All you'd have to do is call the local realtor, put a new roof on the old barn, re-shingle the house, plant some flowers in the dooryard, get rid of that old pile of tires behind the shed, drill a well, put in a new septic system, replace all the windows, blow in some foam insulation, and then sit back and wait for the sale to be complete so you can pay off the loan it took to get the house ready to sell. Then, after you figure in the interest on the loan and the realtor's commission, maybe you'd have enough left from the sale of the property to buy a trailer and, if you're very lucky, a one-acre piece of land in some less desirable town farther from the coast. And once you install yourself and the family in this trailer, then you'll have all the time in the world, time you would have wasted working the land, to figure out how to earn a living so you can pay your ever-rising property taxes. Not to mention the capital gains tax due on the sale of your desirable property, which cost you nothing since it was family land but brought a good price on the market for its "possible view" if all the pines are cut down and no condominiums are constructed between it and the view. So you sit back in your vinyl dinette chair, crank open the tiny window over the sink, and watch the flypaper sway in the breeze. This is really living! Let the new owner take care of all those falling-down buildings. Except they aren't falling down anymore because you broke your back and your bank account fixing everything up before you left for good. So, see? This is what can happen without an effective and up-to-date dose of Serum B.

But before I get carried away with my madness, let me get back to the root cause of the problem I'm railing against. Maybe it's because my antibodies are just as fresh as they can be, but I'm sick of hearing LAND referred to as a commodity like any other. I'm sick of the logic that disparages land that's just sitting there not doing anything. Undeveloped land is a waste, they say. Farm land is, too. Leave farming to the big midwestern conglomerates. This land here is too nice for farming. And you have a right, even an obligation, to invest your money in a growth industry. Money is what the economy needs, not farming.

Now take this land, I can hear them say, the plaid and the pin-striped standing by the edge of the road with the white Jeep still idling. Once it was a pasture. But now that the farmer has sold off his cows to pay his taxes, it seems to me that housing is unquestionably the highest and best use of this otherwise wasted resource. Especially second homes. Just look at that view! Of course, affordable housing is important, too, for those who can afford it. And not only that, small towns like these, where farming is already a thing of the past, provide the most efficient location for capital investment since their Land-Use Ordinances are scarcely understood by their own citizens, and we do have our lawyers if it should come to that. And besides, this town needs development. You'd be doing them a favor. Think of the benefits from the increased tax revenues. The town will be taking in so much more money that they'll easily afford all the new services that development will demand. A new school, town hall, firehouse, better roads, isn't that what they've always wanted, after all? And think of the tide of commercial development that inevitably must follow, a whole new area for investment! A 7-11 store where the dairy farm used to be, a video store and laundromat where they cut down the old orchard. So many new jobs available, so much more money flowing into the local economy, so many new cars, refrigerators, lawnmowers.

Oh yes, I know what you're thinking. I can be mean and ornery when the flies are buzzing, no doubt about it. But just to show you my humanitarian side, let me get back to the proposal I began with. Mainers, both born and adopted, face serious financial pressures due to rising property values, and these pressures threaten to render blackfly serum ineffective. And so I propose a new Ordinance that will at least soften the effect of land sales. What I say is, if a developer wants to buy land in this town, who am I to stop him? But before he will be permitted to re-sell the acreage, he must fulfill the following eight requirements. To whit:

ONE, that he must first reside on said LAND for a period of at least twelve months, before any further subdivision and/or sale thereof occurs;

TWO, that the residency be exclusive, that is, simultaneous ownership of no other residence be permitted;

THREE, that he construct such shelter as necessary for survival from native materials available on the site, using hand tools;

FOUR, that he grow or forage on the site such food as necessary for survival;

FIVE, that he amend the soil by the addition of at least five cubic yards per 1000 square feet of compost, manure, peat, and/or other organic materials;

SIX, that he plant one apple or other fruit-bearing tree or bush for every twenty trees felled on the property;

SEVEN, that he be required to serve on at least one town committee, preferably the Budget Committee or Solid Waste Committee, and further that he attend *all* meetings of one of the following governing boards: Selectmen, School Board, or Planning Board;

EIGHT, that he participate in all legally constituted public Bean Suppers, being in attendance for the full period in which beans are served, and remaining after the last seating to help restore the Grange hall to its previous state of cleanliness and order.

With this system in place, the developer will receive at least the first doses of the blackfly serum which will render him immune to his own arguments. He will begin to mutter "I have the land, I have the land" as he tosses in his sleeping bag with mosquitoes whining in his ear, and slowly, over the course of the four seasons on his new land, he will begin to understand this phrase in the inoculated way. Soon he'll be sending for his family, and together they'll be constructing a more permanent shelter in which to live. They'll be out tilling the fields early in April, before the first onslaught of flies, and then later, equipped with bug nets and fly dope, they'll be bending toward the earth with the devotion of the native. As their hands open up the soil and drop the seeds into it, they will finally realize what "I have the land" really means, and the long process of saving the land, the land that has always sustained us, will have begun.

Lord Love a Swamp

1990

*In visions & dreams I have swept away the
slash from the woods, taken down pines & poplars
& cherries that grow like weeds. But the reality is
that each of those pieces of wood is heavy, stub-
born, and cutting them down produces large,
clumsy, unsightly brush piles which are difficult
& time-consuming to move. Ah, visions!*

—Diary entry, 6/10/77

I came here to get away from it all, and I mean ALL, and yet
little by little I've had to accept the way things really are. That's
the difference between being 30 and being 45. At 30, you've just
finished being 20, only now you have the means to DO what you've
been dreaming of ever since you were 10. At 30, if you're the frugal
type, you've had a chance to save some money, and you've had time
to find someone who shares your dream and your savings account.
At 30, if you're a woman, you might still be teetering on the
edge of reproductivity, listening attentively to the ticking of the
biological clock, and when you hear the alarm go off, the nesting

instinct begins in earnest. Which is where that savings account
comes in, because nests cost money. It was when our baby was on
the way that we got the first hint of what the world really expected
of us.

"You'll have to get electricity," the nurse said in the same breath
as she announced to us that I was pregnant. "Here, my husband's
an electrician, here's his card."

Shocked, we stumbled out of the doctor's office, the first one
we'd been in since we became hippies except for the time I needed
a few stitches from a saw-cut, and had to put up with a lecture
from the emergency room doctor: "How Can an Educated Woman
Like You Live Like a Savage and Without Medical Insurance." But
this time we took our new doctor's advice seriously because we had
scouted him out as being something of a hippie himself. We'd
wanted a home-birth, and the local midwives' group said he was
the one, but it turned out he would not do a birth in a home without running water and electricity. We agreed to a natural birth in
the hospital, which sounds like a contradiction but never mind,
and because he respected our values, we tried to do what he said.
We left the office and drove our faded red VW to the nearest super-
market for the first time in years, and bought milk, real milk, not
the powdered kind we'd been using, and a piece of liver. We made
it back to our overgrown acres just in time for my first bout of nau-
sea.

"Gee, I knew having a kid would change things," said my bewildered husband that evening as he cooked the liver while I tried
to keep from throwing up, "but I thought we had eight more months."

That's the trouble with dreams. They have very little to do
with reality. Maybe that first doctor was right. At least if you buy
into the "system" you don't have to suffer the brutal pain of disillu-
sionment. Anyway, we did have eight more months, and we tried

not to change our routines just for the sake of a perfectly natural phenomenon like birth. Eight months is a long time, especially when you're hauling water every day, planting the usual huge garden, harvesting and canning right up to the due date, and fending off grandparental concern about how we plan to raise a child without running water, electricity, a nursery, a bathtub, a washing machine, a refrigerator, none of which we had at the time, nor planned to have EVER. I'd always admired the simplicity of nature, and I hadn't noticed any of these modern conveniences in the woods, but then chipmunks don't go to college either, so what did I expect? The stitches-doctor was right. If you're educated, nothing is ever simple, least of all simplicity.

All I can say is that a little self-imposed hardship can go a long way toward making you an ornery cuss. Even when you soften your life a bit, succumbing to your own fatigue, you never forget what it was like to wring out those cloth diapers and load them into a bushel basket for the weekly trip to the laundromat. You never forget grinding the flour for your baby's pablum, or the way you wore him on your back as you hauled water for a few more years before calling it quits. Everything you do, after such a life, has the flavor of all you've been through to arrive at what little comfort you can now afford. When Chris said, "You deserve it," he knew all about the chosen life in the woods. He wasn't just trying to cheer me up the way our attorney tried the day we sat in his office with the white-Jeep-realtor in the plaid shirt. It had come to that, you see. We weren't going to let a developer mess with a couple of old hippies and turn the woods across the road into his proposed nine-lot subdivision. Oh no, we'd rather jump through the ultimate hoop of the 'eighties, ornery cusses though we were, and take out our first bank loan, after engaging for years in the subversive activity of paying cash for everything. We bitterly

handed over a check for the "lot" across the road. A check, I might
mention, that amounted to more than I earn in a year, which says
either that I don't make very much, which is true, or that we paid
dear for that tangle of trees, which is also true.

"It's ironic," I commented to the lawyer as I let go of that thin
slip of paper, "that today's the day our hot water heater was in-
stalled. We have hot running water now!"

"You deserve it," he responded, echoing Chris' words of support. "If you're going to have condominiums across the road, you
might as well have hot water."

Another dose of reality medicine. But I can still dream, can't I?
Why else "own" woods, if not to let them act as a buffer between
what you want and what you are. No matter how hard you will
ever work, you can never gain control over a wild wood, which
teaches you something about human effort and the grandiosity of a
life's plan. I like to think the woods represent a limit to the hu-
manly possible, a place where you can talk all you want but you'll
never convince the trees to obey. Dey no speak-a da language. You
can fool yourself when it comes to housebuilding, where once you
nail a board into place, it pretty much stays where you put it. But
lumber, like me, is already a few steps removed from its primitive
origins. Like me, it's been through the mill.

The woods dose me with another kind of reality medicine, a
tonic that restores my faith in our simple beginnings. I feared I'd
forsaken that simplicity the day I finally heard a refrigerator hum-
ming in my kitchen for the first time, on our son's fifth birthday.
Don't get me wrong. I love ice cubes and cold beer, and not having
to go down cellar to get last night's leftovers. And from Noah's
point of view, four birthdays without ice cream was enough. A refrigerator is one of the most necessary of luxuries, and one of the
most luxurious of necessities, using up as much power in one day

as our whole photovoltaic home uses in two. But I have my fanatic husband to thank once again for managing to run a very efficient, tightly insulated refrigerator, lights, a TV and VCR, a water pump, and power tools on sixteen solar panels. Pretty good for a couple of would-be zucchini farmers.

And yet the woods beckon me to leave all that behind. Before we came to Maine to live the simple life, I would sometimes get so fed up with civilization that I'd launch into what Kal calls my "cave speech." He would brace himself for my shouting, "I'm going to go live in a cave! I'll dress in animal skins, I'll eat wild greens, I'll cut myself off from complicity with this world!" I didn't go live in a cave, but I do find solace in a wild place, so after our visit to the lawyer's that day I went walking in the woods we'd just gone into debt to buy. The realtor, sliding our check into his plaid pocket, had declared that his client, the developer, was doing us a big favor to sell us this lot. He could have gotten more for it, he said, but he wanted good relations with the abutters. A wise decision, given the vociferous nature of these particular abutters.

We'd already gone, well prepared, to the Planning Board hearing, much to the developer's surprise. Along with our neighbors, we'd argued that our one-lane dirt road could most certainly not, based on experience at backing up or pulling off into the ditch when we saw another vehicle coming, handle the proposed nine new house-lots. Kal and I led the charge, employing the measured terms we'd learned in our years as dean and professor, in which one never mentions the pronoun "I" or breathes even a hint that the concern may have an ounce of connection to one's own very heart and soul, but is, rather, a philosophical question whose resolution will serve as a precedent for future generations. In short, we tried to be rational.

And there was no scarcity of evidence to support our rationality. We brought in a diagram of the road, showing the various blind spots, the average width of ten feet, the places where the ice never melts and then the spring mud makes the road nearly impassable. Think of the increased traffic nine new houses would entail, we argued. How long would it be before the newcomers, innocent of the one-lane rules evolved by the four families now living up there, would cause a serious collision? How long would it be before a child was hit? How would the town pay for the damage that such volume of traffic would cause to the road in mud season, when even now we sometimes had to walk in from the main road? How long would it be before the new owners came to the Selectmen, demanding a wider road, a paved road, and at what cost to the town? How long before they demanded school bus pick-up at the door instead of down at the main road, and at what cost to the town? Besides these anecdotal persuasions, we also took recourse to the Subdivision Ordinance itself, citing the official requirements pertaining to road safety, which of course could never be met by our little towpath. We were so well-prepared it was downright embarrassing. But then, they don't call me professor for nothing.

I admit that what I really wanted the Planning Board to say was You are absolutely right, and what we're going to do is keep that acreage as a nature preserve, with you as the warden. Not to worry—the developer was only kidding. We put him up to it, just to make sure you townspeople were paying attention.

But of course, reality has a nasty way of not being able to take a joke. In fact the Board's response was equally rational, and even true. You just don't want more people up there in your woods, they asserted, knowing as well as we did that the Ordinance doesn't cover that. Road safety isn't really what concerns you, and you know it, they contested. Why, if the road conditions are really so hazardous, you should have moved out of there a long time ago. No one should live on a road like that, if all you're telling us is so. NO ONE should live up there, and that's a fact. But since it's dangerous already, new lots won't make it any more dangerous, though nine does sound like lots of lots. We'll limit the developer to four, and hope for the best.

Does it surprise you that the developer wants to maintain good relations with these abutters so skilled at rebuttal? Of course he'll take a loss to sell us one of the lots, since otherwise he may get stuck with an indivisible 80-acre chunk of, heaven forbid, useless land. But when I came home and walked into our 17-acre share, I wondered if we were the fools who'd done the favor. I found that the only possible building site on the property was submerged under water, and this was October. Just imagine it in April. No house lot, this. Land that only an abutter could love. Or a duck. I trudged through the muck, clambered over old slash piles left from a long-ago logging operation, keeping the sun over my right shoulder so I wouldn't get lost, but it clouded over and I soon found myself without so much as an orange surveyor's tape to show me the boundary. It's all in how you define reality, I guess, if the hated orange tape can suddenly become your salvation.

Okay, I said to myself, climbing up onto a boulder to catch my breath. Okay, so I'm lost. I just happen to have these dried apricots in my pocket, so I'll sit here and listen to the squirrels chattering high in the hemlocks. I'll look around at the natural disarray of the scene. Trees so crowded they bear leaves only at the crown. Many fallen trees. Dead trunks riddled with woodpecker holes. Tiny oak saplings clustered at the base of giant old ones. Boulders only a glacier could move, and water collecting in algae-covered pools. What a wonderfully useless place this is! I'm not even tempted to use that fancy "could-be" vision of mine on this tangled place. No way could I clean up these fallen limbs, gather these boulders into a wall, prune these trees, cultivate watercress in that stream, make a path. There is, here, another vision of order, free from human dominance. You would have to call it ugly. I think I *will* call it ugly, and love its ugliness as the safeguard of its preservation. I paid good money to "own" this place that does not need me, this place immune to settlement, this place that contains nothing anyone would want to buy. *That* is surely worth a year's salary!

I feel a surge of my "cave mentality," suddenly exhilarated to have spent money on something that will never pay me back. I've removed this piece of land from the currency of use and value exchange. I've erased it from the realtors' maps once and for all. I let loose a wild shriek, scaring the squirrels one story higher into the hemlocks. I slide down from the boulder, delighted to have found at last this *real* estate, and . . . what's that? I squint through a space in the trees, spying something odd there, something starkly rectangular, something familiar . . . but what is it? I jump back with surprise and, I confess, relief when I see it's my own dining room window! I'm not lost at all. I'm home!

I scramble over boulders and branches, bruised and breathless, and reach the blessed road. I go inside and brew some tea. Holding the warm mug, I lean against the windowsill seeing what it IS I'm looking at, not what it could be. I sigh, content. I have exchanged money to save a wilderness in the name of love.

The Rockland That Was

1995

When we came here, I liked to think of this land as the place
where history came to die. But I was younger then. I firmly believed that partridges, owls, and whip-poor-wills had more of a right
to this patch of wilderness than I had, but that if I promised to love
the land, they would let me settle here and raise my vegetables
and my child. What did I know about history? By now I've learned
there's something discouragingly eternal about it, if history means
human action on the face of the earth. No whip-poor-will singing
on a branch at dusk can compete with the force of human change.

Take Rockland, our nearest major town. Back in 1977, Rockland
was a quiet coastal town, a town without pretense, a town without
a single fancy restaurant, or anyplace to buy the *New York Times*,
or anyone who'd want to. A town that often stank of fish because
that was the local industry. A poor town, yes, a seafaring town that
had seen better days. This was a town where the neon "Jesus Saves"
was the brightest thing on Route One, where on Saturday nights a
trail of cars and trucks led right to the local Bean Supper, and by

ten o'clock, only the blinking yellow light at the corner would still be awake.

You came to Rockland because you needed something like rubber boots or lumber, or if you cut your hand sawing down a tree and had to see a doctor. You came to Rockland on a rainy day because it was freezing in the trailer you were living in while you built your house, and it was too muddy for moving rocks or breaking sod in your freshly plowed ground, so you might as well go to the laundromat and keep warm beside the driers. You came to Rockland to see a movie, if you didn't mind last year's hits, or to eat a tuna sandwich and potato salad, heavy on the mayonnaise, at the local coffee shop and wonder if you'd ever be part of this close-knit community where six or eight surnames seemed to fill half the skinny little phone book. You came to Rockland, in short, because you needed it as much as it needed you, and you were in it together, for life. And you never, no matter which musty old store on Main Street with a high tin ceiling and dark wood floor you went into, you never saw a single bright-red plastic lobster or blueberry ashtray.

Now I'm a lot older, and while I still raise a huge garden, and spend a lot of time moving rocks and building things, I guess I've changed with the times in spite of myself. I like to buzz into town and sit in a nice café with art on the walls. I'd be lying if I said it was all romance, the old days, living on the land, kerosene lamps and woodstoves, hauling water and eating rhubarb or rutabagas each in its season, and coming to Rockland only to buy nails. If I look up from my seat in the café, I can still see the high tin ceiling, and beneath my feet is the old wood floor. But this isn't a hardware store anymore. And I'm worried—another product of being older, I suppose. I'm worried about our choices, all of ours, because a croissant is nice, but nails are necessary, nails hold things together. I think about the old settlers, and the long journey it was for them to travel to the county seat, Rockland, in a horse and wagon. It took a whole day, and they went there to trade: a barrel of flour for a barrel of nails, potatoes for fish. I trade money for pastries. I'm uneasy about these changes, these choices.

For them, life wasn't choices. Life was life. You did what you had to do, to survive. Maybe that's what I meant when I thought this was the place where history came to die. History is about progress, not just survival. History is about leaving our mark. The old settlers' mark is a bunch of tilting gravestones and some broken-down stone walls, and I wonder if, as they heaved rocks into intricately fitted walls, they thought about us, the future, or were they just trying to get these stones the hell out of the field. Whatever their motive, they left a mark with their lives. And we leave one with ours.

I look around the once-wild, now half-tamed place I call home. I promised that whip-poor-will I'd love the land, and make it better. Let the orchard testify for me, and the rebuilt stone walls, the lilies and the asparagus patch, the reddest of rhubarb. But what mark have I left with the vow to honor the small town that needed me, the Rockland that was? I have trouble admitting that even though I arrived before "the boom," and brought my own compost in the back of a pick-up truck, I am part of what transformed the sleepy midcoast of Maine forever. But then, that's another thing I've learned as I've gotten older, that all my actions are part of larger actions, that I have a hand in this progress called history.

I used to think the hand that wields the hoe does nothing but bring forth beans. Not so. If it weren't for my rows of beans, this place would be years closer to being a pine forest. If it weren't for the beans grown by all of us who came here to live on the land, to find jobs or start our own businesses, to buy supplies in town, to give birth to children, to vote at Town Meeting for the roads and services we need to sustain our lives, perhaps Rockland would still be sleeping peacefully in a fogbank, forgotten by time. I promised that whip-poor-will I'd always eat beans, and I never go back on my word to a bird. But beans carry a price-tag along with everything else.

Even Stones Dissolve in the Rain

1984

Sometimes, when I step out at night and hear the
wind tickling the poplar leaves, I realize the life of
this land was going on long before I ever came
here to make my home. Night and day the moon
and sun rose and set, winds whirled, leaves grew
& died, the road curved up around the corner
toward the big oak in the dark. This place
contains me and my little life now.

—Diary entry, 8/30/77

The past never dies. It seeps into the land we inhabit. Then lilacs bloom to remind us every spring that time is not a straight line denying recurrence. Bluets spill over the ground and apple trees are covered with blossoms, lilies shoot up and maple leaves unfurl. Human history is nothing but a transparency laid over what recurs in nature.

Yes, trees get bigger. Old ones die, split open by their own weight. Young ones spring up. You can't have things always exactly the same. Even the planets and stars shift imperceptibly from year to year. Even stones dissolve in the rain.

Human history remains the same, too, though that's harder to perceive. The idea of progress makes us forget that the most essential elements of life remain the same. We're so proud of our modern inventions, our easier life. We think our age is so remarkably different from, say, a hundred years ago. But humans are no different from maple trees. We grow and adapt. Old ones die. Young ones sprout. The surroundings may change, but birth, life, and death stay the same.

When lilacs bloom I am inspired, like Walt Whitman, to remember the dead who once lived on this ridge, as I do for now. My young son and I make a pilgrimage to the old cemetery down the road. I sit in the fullness of quiet, gazing at the old headstones and the huge maple tree. I watch apple-blossom petals fall lightly on the graves while my son runs around on the grass. Sometimes we bring our lunch. Coming here in the midst of our living is a sacrament. Eating peanut butter sandwiches in sight of the dead reminds me that we are alive and mutable. We breathe, eat, and sleep. We grow older.

It seems like a long time, this span of a human life, and yet it is the blink of an eye. I recall chatting with the local garage mechanic about my son's birth and his daughter's leaving for college. "Ayuh," he said, "you bring 'em home from the hospital, and next thing you know they're gettin' on the school bus, and when they get off they're seniors."

And yet time is slow and long, too. I could occupy myself forever with the memories and experiences of my short span of life. The day my own grandfather was buried, when I was 12, seems so dim it could be some story I read in a book. But being here in the old cemetery resurrects buried feelings of puzzlement and finality. I want to penetrate the darkness of these graves and make the people spring up again like bluets. While my son chases butterflies, I run my fingers over the gravestones, reading the inscriptions like Braille.

Julia and Paul Metcalf died in their 80's, outliving their daughters Olive, Emily and Eunice, who all died of smallpox in 1848. The girls were 20, 15, and 13. I let my imagination water these engraved facts, and what germinates is the helplessness, anger, sadness, and resignation Julia and Paul must have felt. After the burial, when all the neighbors finally left, they sit in the twilight, quietly rocking on the porch. Then Paul gets up to milk the cows and Julia goes inside. Her eyes alight on the mending pile, but now she won't need to mend the skirts or stockings of her daughters. Now there are no more children, and there will be no grandchildren either. The silence of these refused generations pervades the darkened house. Julia lights the lamp and sits down to darn Paul's socks. The feet of the living, feet that can still wear a hole in a sock, comfort her. Her needle flashes back and forth. Work helps her mend the hole in her heart as her daughters lie quietly asleep under ground.

Julia and Paul were not the only neighbors to suffer this loss. Junie and Melinda Metcalf lost their 3-year-old Harriet, too. It was a bad year, and by the end of 1848 nearly all the children were dead. Life just went out of the young ones, leaving the parents to carry on for 40 or 50 more years. But with no children or grandchildren, to what purpose was their laboring? There would be no son or daughter to take over the farm. Before too long, trees creep back into the fields, dug wells go dry, houses burn, cellars cave in. And only the headstones tell the tale.

But a headstone doesn't tell much of a tale. It tells more than a cellarhole or a dry well. At least a grave gives a few facts: who, when, and sometimes how they died. So many questions remain. History is a fiction created by those who survive.

Bartholomew Sukeforth was 71 when he died in 1890, and his wife Rhoda made it to the twentieth century, dying in 1908 at 80. But their 17-year-old son Philip died in 1865. Was he a Civil War casualty? Or did he fall off the hay wagon and die of a concussion? And what happened in 1866, when another batch of children died? John, Mary, and Lora Skinner, all under 3 years old, lie alone in their tiny graves. Their parents are not buried here. Did they flee the farm, despondent, moving to town to find work that didn't need a next generation? Did they want to forget the horror of three dead children buried by the edge of the woods?

And what of one-month-old Little Nelle, another victim of 1866? I can almost feel the fullness of her mother's breasts, swollen with milk and grief. A headstone doesn't tell me this, but I am a mother and I know.

Or Mary Lassell. She died at 34, in 1859. She left two children, Olive, 9, and Paul, 3. Their tears of abandonment are not recorded on the stone. But both children died three years later. What did they die of? Motherlessness?

Here in the cemetery the compression of time gives me compassion. Facts make us feel separate from olden times, but feeling unites us. I may wear jeans and sneakers, while the women buried here wore heavy long skirts and high laced boots. I may give peanut butter sandwiches to my son, but they fed their children too, while they had them. They too watched apple-blossoms scatter pale petals in the breeze, and smiled as their children danced around the maple trees. And then they buried their children under lilies. Will I be called upon to do this too?

Human history sings its familiar refrain. Progress, invention, facts, are etchings on stone. Even stones dissolve in the rain. Birth, life, and death remain ever the same.

THE WORLD

"The phone is connected, at last—
a convenience, an intrusion. Sometimes
it rings and I don't answer. It stops,
and I'm back in my wilderness again,
just where I want to be."

—Diary entry, 10/28/77

George's Store

1989

One old verity of country life is the general store, which is typically almost as old as the town itself. Ours is green, and it's starting to buckle and cave in as it leans away from the road. The front door yawns and stretches toward the back room where Georgie used to eat his bologna sandwich and do the books. Changes in the store marked our passage through time from newcomer to the status of old-comer as clearly as the birth and growth of our son gave Georgie a friendly yardstick to measure us by.

"My he's growing!" the old bachelor storekeeper would croon as Noah reached his little hands up to the glass cabinet that housed the candy bars we never ate and the razorblades my bearded husband never used. "'Twasn't but yestiddy he was a babe in arms!"

Back before Noah was born and we used to go to the movies at night sometimes, we'd drive by and see the bare bulb shining through the grimy front window of the closed store. "Georgie's at it again," we'd joke, picturing the small man licking the end of his pencil and counting on his fingers the cans of corn he'd sold that day, and the ones he still had on the shelves. He wrote a receipt for every purchase, no matter how small, arduously spelling out each item in a 19th-century schoolboy hand, spidery and illegible as if written on a slate in some long-forgotten schoolroom that smelled of chalk, kerosene, and woodsmoke. And he would hand you the carbon copy as he placed the items gently into a carton from his pile of nested boxes behind the counter. The original copy he'd save, pierced by a spindle next to the cash register, to aid his midnight tally.

While Georgie labored over your receipt, it seemed like the whole town would be lined up behind you waiting their turn, exchanging the day's gossip. George's Store was a third-class post office, too, so at eleven every morning there was always a big crowd. Third-class means he sorted the mail into glass cubbies behind the counter, and you had to ask for it. We had our own zip code, even though the town didn't appear on any map of Maine that I ever saw. Those were the days before the surge of junk mail, luckily. It already took him most of the morning to sort a canvas pouch of mail into the 50 little cubbies. We got the last one when we moved here. Otherwise you'd have to wait till someone died, I guess. He knew where everyone lived, even all the new hippies who settled back in the woods. He called us all by name.

The government has phased out third-class post offices as all the old postmasters like Georgie retired from those general stores, the kind with oiled wood floors as black as boots, and bare bulbs hanging from the high tin ceiling. There was nothing electronic about those stores. The cash register's numbers would rise in a window like moons at the press of a key. Scales had weights at one end. The old chest freezer had frost so thick that only one row of juice cans could fit. Oil-cloth covered the shelves, and a graceful arc of letters in the front window said TETLEY TEA. In later years it said   ETLEY   A. Outside there was an old metal sign with a rusty Wonder Bread kid, grinning his rusty smile. And of course there was a Coca-Cola thermometer right by the torn and sagging screen door.

Georgie would always comment on the weather, though he only got out in it twice a day, walking down the sloped path from his house across the road at 6 a.m. and back up again at 7 p.m. Saturday nights he baked his own beans, just for himself. He was proud of that. On Sundays he was closed.

Now weeds grow out of the cracked pavement in front that used to be for parking. Many a loud greeting or long tale was exchanged out there, but now it's all chicory and crickets. " EORGE'S TOR ," the sign says, to no one in particular. Now we each have our own mailbox along the roadside, and we don't see each other as much anymore. We have a new local store, though, an electronic one, with a Megabucks machine by the door. Georgie would never have sold lottery tickets. Can't get somethin for nothin, he would have said. He couldn't sell beer, with the post office there, not that he would have. Georgie didn't sell pizza, either, or rent movies. That was before everyone, or anyone, had a VCR. He didn't even sell sandwiches, but you could get a loaf of white bread, a pound of bologna tied in paper with a string, and a jar of French's mustard, to make your own the way he always did. He wasn't big on lettuce, and only a few brown bananas and some limp carrots sat on a forgotten dusty shelf over the freezer. Most everything he sold was canned, and sometimes he still had products they don't even make anymore, sometimes even for the old price, say 19 cents for a crock-shaped jar of B & M Baked Beans. He was too busy to mark things up, or rotate the stock. He was too busy to have a life of his own, spent so much time on his midnight inventories. "Sold three cans of tomato soup today, four jars of Skippy, and a box of macaroni, four dozen hot dogs and ten loaves of bread," I can picture him muttering, writing it out one letter at a time into his old ledger, a diary of sorts. And then he'd yank on the string to turn off the swinging lightbulb, pull the warped door hard behind him, and head across the road for a few hours of sleep before opening again at 6 a.m. I don't know why he opened so early. He didn't even sell hot coffee. Not a single styrofoam cup ever crossed his worn old threshold.

Now we have a vacant store in what used to be the center of what used to be a town, an ample building with a big attached barn right at the four corners of two slow roads, right smack in the middle of nowhere, just going to waste. In the eight years since Georgie closed his store and post office, and went up the sloping path to his house one last time, and went inside to rock by the window and bake his beans, this town, like the rest of the country, has gone into waste in a big way. Our new store, a mile down the road from Georgie's corner, started out as a tiny shack that sold mostly candy and chips, with an old white refrigerator filled with soda just outside the door. Then they added bread and milk. Then, after Georgie retired, they built a full store and moved the original building out back for bottle redemptions. Put in a long line of silver coolers filled with beer. Canned goods. A meat counter. Then a dairy freeze. Video games. Gas pumps. Pizza and sandwiches, now, too.

And styrofoam plates and cups. And plastic bags. And aluminum wrappers. And those rings that hold together six-packs. And little juice bottles. I know, because when I'm out walking I find a lot of this stuff drifting onto the sides of the road. It's not as quiet as it once was. Especially not on Friday and Saturday nights, when all the cars in town crowd into the parking lot, and people line up to get their pizza, beer and soda, tonight's movie, gas, and a little chat. But I'm not knocking it. A small town needs a place like that.

It used to be the dump that served as the weekend gathering spot. But now there's no more socializing with neighbors as we jettison our junk into the ditch. No more coming home from the dump with as much as we went with. Now we each set our pre-paid trash bags out by the roadside, and we watch through the window, sipping our solitary coffee, as the truck carries our trash away at a dollar a bag. A dollar now, that is. Soon it will be more, much much more, and we will have to recycle whether we believe in it or not.

I, for one, do believe in it. I'm an old hippie just itchy to re-cycle. And whenever I drive by George's vacant store, where the sign over the door now reads only " GE ," an old hippie fantasy is kindled in my mind.

Why not turn GEORGE'S STORE into a town recycling center?

There'd be bins and barrels and boxes for different colored glass, aluminum, plastic. There'd be stacks of newspaper and piles of collapsed cardboard boxes. Newsletters and posters would crowd the walls and windows. We could even have classes in home waste management, backyard composting, energy conservation. The boy scouts and girl scouts, the 4-H, the Grange, the organic gardeners, everyone could get together at GEORGE'S STORE, just like in the old days, and learn to make use of the mounds of trash that we might not even be dealing with today if stores like George's had stayed open. Stores like George's were just one step up from somebody's pantry. They sold what you needed, no more, and usu-ally less. Who needed a better product than the good chat to be had back in the old old days, when Georgie's father ran the store and everyone would sit around with their feet propped up on the rail of the pot-bellied stove? Maybe, if we could go back in time, we could retrieve some of the other ways of the old general store, too, like tying the meat up with paper (recycled, of course) and string. Or scooping our groceries out of bins and weighing them into brown bags. Or wrapping our choice of in-season, locally grown produce in old newspaper.

This begins to sound dangerously like a co-op store, don't you think? And I've been around here long enough to know such ideas don't go down easy in this little town. Believe me, I'm not saying that hippie days are here again. Hippies are a thing of the past, they tell me. But, in my years as one, I've come to know this about natural cycles: what goes around comes around, and that includes ideas. The back-to-the-land movement surprised the older generation after all they'd done for their children, giving us what they never had, putting hardships of Depression and World War II behind them. Our arrival in towns like this one made the old-timers scratch their head, and yet they watched with fond nostalgia as we reconstructed the simpler ways they'd left behind. They warmed to our how-to questions: how to store carrots and potatoes in a cellar, how to salt down cabbage, how to keep a cookstove going all through a subzero night, how to dowse for water. We helped them remember the good things that are also lost when you try so hard to forget the bad.

But hardship isn't the worst that can happen. Their economic trials may appear light compared to the real risk of wasting our planet. Before stores like George's turn to compost themselves, starting with the rotting old sills, ideas as old as nature return. Remember I said I used to think this was the place where history came to die? I was wrong. History lives in us, even if we refuse the responsibility. You can't go live in a cave. I know, because I've tried it. You can't say NO to unsolved human problems anymore, even in this small town, and that's what the story of our mounting trash is all about. You can't bury it, and though the regional incinerator continues to burn it for now, there is no place to dump the ash. It's costing more and more money to avoid the issues, and the one good thing that money does is, it talks. It talks and people listen, and then we start saying YES to change.

Of course, I'd be the first to admit that I only support saying YES to change that goes backward, kind of like the way George's Store leans away from the road.

Wheaten Loaf

1990

Small town Mainers joke about mosquitoes in their season, but the subject of loving jest in March is mud. We delight in the ooze that marks the end of the freeze even if it means being up to our axles in it. When the frost in the dirt roads lets go, an event usually coinciding with Town Meeting just so we'll have something to complain about when the topic of roads comes up, it's a sure sign of spring though two more chilly months must pass before the trees leaf out. One rule of Mainer behavior is never relish the pleasures of one season without warning of the pain to come in the next one.

"Nice spring day, idn't it?"

"Ayuh, won't be long now 'fore the flies hatch."

Town Meeting Day is not always a nice spring day. But if it is, it's with sorrow that you climb into the car, heading for a hard wooden chair and the droning litanies of democracy, instead of slogging out to the garden in high boots to see if the chives are up, or maybe moving a few rocks or raking up the old dog droppings that lie moldering on the dead grass. If it is a nice day, melting snow will be trickling in rivulets down the middle of the muddy backroads so that, looking around the Town Hall parking lot, you can tell by the mud-covered hubcaps who lives where. Since mine are brown all the way up to the "Toyota," you can guess I live way back in, and this fact can be used to predict my politics—whether I'll vote aye or nay on road maintenance today.

Or Town Meeting Day might be morosely grey and drizzly, verging on freezing, and as you drive through town, you see smoke curling from every chimney, all the fires in town well stoked and banked for the long, long day ahead. Our town prides itself on having a long, long Town Meeting, the longest one in the county. Reporters from the local paper never stay long enough to find out what really makes us tick. In fact, they usually don't even last through lunchtime. They find it discouraging that by noon we've only managed to argue our way through the long list of funding requests from area social service agencies and have just begun to tackle the school budget. Most towns "aye" the social services with a wave of right hands, but in our town we like to know what we're paying for. Generally we end up saying "aye" to all but the Maine Publicity Bureau because we figure any tourists who really want to find us will manage without state aid, and why should we pay to lure them where we don't even want them? By noon, the reporters have had enough of our cussed independence, so they take their steno pads and cameras over to the next town, where the citizens are just setting down to their bean dinner. We gave up the "bean dinner" at Town Meeting a few years back since our afternoon agenda promises plenty of its own gas.

This time Town Meeting Day dawns drizzly, so better don extra warm clothes. Especially so this year, since one of the agenda items published in the Town Report calls for a new furnace in the Town Hall, and the Selectmen are sure to leave the old one turned off just to make their point. Being a literature professor comes in handy in these matters where it takes a close study of the text to know which way the wind blows and whether to wear a sweater. On second thought, maybe I won't be needing that sweater, since our town prides itself not only on the longest meeting in the county, but the hottest one, too. By noon, furnace or no, the hall will be efficiently heated by recirculated arguments. Recirculated, mind you, and recycled, which puts our town in the forefront of this year's hot new statewide concern. We pride ourselves on re-using the same arguments every year to heat this room where many of the old-timers learned their ABC's, a socio-historical fact which makes the debate over the school budget about as ripe as a meth-ane-rich manure pile.

"Why, this here school was good enough for us," the elderly one-room alumni assert year after year as we watch the budget climb and the literacy rate drop. Actually we only discuss the school budget tangentially in March, and hold a Special Town Meeting in June for the vote, but the morning full of requests from social ser-vice agencies seems to bring us right back to education time and again, just like the farmer who carries grain to the cows then has to muck out their stalls before going in for his pancakes.

"We was taught the hard way," the old-timers say, "we had to do the chores and that. We didn't have time for drugs, even if there'd been any. Our daddy would whup us good if we was caught smokin behind the barn."

And yet the majority, unconvinced, responds by voting tax dol-lars to help solve the complex network of modern problems, the reason the kids are having a hard time learning even in the brand-new school that the old-timers tried to vote down a few years back. The nay-sayers don't stand a chance against the answering coali-tion of their own grown children, the latest crop of newcomers who run more to the Yuppie variety, and the old crop of newcomers whom

I call old-comers, a rugged bunch of middle-aged hippies who've refused to sell out. The antiphony continues, the gasses heat up, the gavel resounds, "Please address your comments to the moderator!" and finally, saved by the bell, the two hands on the clock jerk to the 12, and lunchtime holds out the promise of peace.

We don't have a "bean dinner" at Town Meeting anymore, but we still adhere to the healing powers of communal eating. Lunchtime finds everyone all smiles as neighbors turn jovially to neighbors, commenting on the pageantry and performance of the morning session. Hard feelings are forgotten as chairs scrape back and everyone presses out of the stuffy room to the waiting sandwiches. Stacks of sandwiches, each in a plastic bag, ham salad and tuna salad and egg salad and peanut butter with grape jelly, all on white bread, the same choices every year, sold to fund the tiny Town Library. And a table of cookies, and a table of drinks in styrofoam cups, all laid out as it was from the beginning of time. In lunch, as in all else at Town Meeting except for the problems, everything is as it always was, everything is as it should be.

The conversation, too, follows the same rhythms every year, where the morning's arguments are forgotten and everyone has a story to share from over the winter, about frozen pipes or the barn roof caving in or the day the blizzard hit and the cows got out. You know the kind of story I mean, old fictions that might have been told around the pickle barrel at the old general store. Except now we don't have the pickle barrel, nor the general store. These are stories that might have been told of a weekend morning, leaning on the tailgate of your truck down at the dump. Except now we don't have a dump anymore either. So these are stories that can only be told here, at Town Meeting, holding a soft white sandwich in one hand and a styrofoam cup in the other.

But wait, something is different this first year that we don't have our dump anymore. Something is very very odd this time, and I'll bet you anything the reporters missed it. I almost missed it myself, lulled by my expectation that nothing ever changes in this town. I should have known that when a town loses its most central function, the huge abyss we called our dump, it loses more than its ability to get rid of what it doesn't want by burying it in the ground. When a town loses its dump, it loses its innocence. Now there are consequences to every action, and even something as simple as a Library-Fund lunch must change. Notice that the sandwiches this year are wrapped in wax paper bags, and the coffee is served in china mugs. Notice, too, that some of the sandwiches are on whole wheat bread. Could this, just possibly, be another consequence of the loss of town innocence?

Because, you see, once the dump itself is not as it should be, not the same as it used to be, once our town can no longer bury what we don't want to deal with, then before you know it everything will change. We'll all be voting "aye" to conservation, recycling, sharing, saving, and the downright neighborliness born of hard times. We'll all be growing our own beans, or maybe even wheat, and re-opening the flour mills that used to run off the town's two rivers in the old days. Before you know it, we'll even be agreeing on the school budget. Well, I may be jumping to a heady conclusion here. Hot coffee does this to me. But mark my words. A town without a dump is a town teetering on the abyss called change.

At the smack of the gavel, we reluctantly return to the long agenda that will hold us in our hard chairs until late afternoon. The absent reporters, who missed the only newsworthy item so far—the subtle changes in our lunchtime ritual and the political implications thereof—will also miss the town's greatest drama, the cult of local personalities enacted in the afternoon session by characters in faded plaid shirts who wave the Town Report at each other as they stand again and again, like Jacks-in-the-Box sprung by the crack of the gavel. It's important to note that the plaid shirts are faded, not the crisp L. L. Bean kind, and they have holes in the elbows, frayed collars, and buttons that bulge over bellies. When dressing for Town Meeting, only the oldest clothes will do.

When I was a newcomer, I sat spellbound as these old-timers rehearsed the old script yet again: to spend money or not, to fix it or not, to look into it or not. I found my emotions pulled this way and that as I exercised the critical faculties I naively believed citizenship required. Once I even stood up myself, but the moderator failed to recognize me since I wasn't wearing a plaid shirt. Which is just as well, because now that I'm an old-comer, I know it doesn't mean a thing, it's just an efficient way to heat the hall. Now I'm able to remain serenely equanimous as I savor this year's special performance from the town historian, a retired lawyer who never ever comes to Town Meeting, never even reads the Town Report, but read it this year and, shocked by the present reality, came to sound the alarm. The accounting is all mixed up, he laments, the figures don't jibe, and why are we spending so much on maintaining this run-down heap of a Town Hall, and so little on the old cemeteries where Gladys and Evelyn and Henry are, who used to animate these meetings in their day? Why all this money on drug education and home health care and fire trucks, when spring rains wash out the cemetery road every year and threaten to erode the graves of our founding families? A town is nothing but its history, he contends, waving his well-marked Report, a pencil behind his ear, and sits down.

The play goes on as the agitated historian gives the stage over to the long-suffering road agent. His lines remain the same year after year, no matter who is cast in the part: "It's up to you folks. It's up to you if your roads is passable or not. It's all up to how much you're willin to pay." And those who drive their compact cars to jobs in distant towns every day vote aye to using more salt on the roads, and those who remember the old days of horse-and-sleigh say nay. And those who live on the mountain road in new houses with south-facing windows vote aye to the town maintaining their road now that good taxpayers live on it, because what will happen if there's ever an emergency and someone's house burns down or an ambulance can't get there in time, and the town is slapped with a lawsuit, then what? And the rest vote nay, you should've known that when you came. If you ever wondered what makes a small town tick, know this: It all comes down to the roads.

The town historian, shaking his head sadly, votes nay to it all, nay to every road in town except the cemetery road, which provokes a vociferous old-comer, who just happens to be wearing his plaid shirt, to break the tension in the hall by saying, "He's against maintaining roads for the living, but he's all for building roads for the dead!" The laughter, a full minute of it, greases the creaky wheel, and all the other articles slide through fast, including a huge sum of money to be paid to haul our trash to another town for disposal, money for planting elm trees by the river, money to paint the Town Hall (white), and a go-ahead on plans for a new fire station. Yes, in a town that no longer has a dump or a general store, a good hearty community laugh is a mighty fine old thing.

And so it goes, while outside the tall windows the day grows old and a thin sleet begins to shush against the glass, coating the windshields of all the parked cars with a film of ice, for March is ever March in Maine, year after year, and even as it comes to pass that the white bread is wheatened by a new way of thinking, and plastic bags become a thing of the past, ice will always be ice. We squirm in our seats, old, young, native, new, anxious to get home before the slippery roads, untended as we sit here arguing about them, become so bad we have to miss our supper.

The gavel finally sounds, and we all file out to our crystalline cars, careful on the slick steps, the rickety railing, the descending path. Sleet falls on one and all, and a familiar sound rises up from the parking lot of a town where no one is exempt from taxes, trash, or the closing ritual of scraping windshields.

12 Ways of Looking at Trash

1992

1.

If Wallace Stevens can come up with "Thirteen Ways of Looking at a Blackbird," I see no reason why I can't offer 12 ways of
looking at a black bag. I'd try for 13 myself, but a black trash bag
is less interesting than a blackbird, though more common in our
town now that we have lost our dump. We have to buy our black
bags at the Town Office, complete with a blaze-orange sticker to
prove we've paid to have our trash picked up and delivered to a
transfer station 20 miles distant. The rising cost, both economic
and ecological, of dealing with what we don't want to deal with has
an emotional cost as well. One outlet for stress in these hard cir-
cumstances is the carefree tossing of junk from moving vehicles.
So begin, if you will, by looking at a black bag with an orange sticker
sitting responsibly, even primly, by the roadside on trash pick-up
day, but in the background I want you to picture our rural fields
filled with forlorn junk in search of the lost landfills of yesteryear.

Ah, yesteryear, when the Town Dump was a deep abyss open
for business every Saturday and Sunday. People backed their loaded

pick-up trucks to the very edge, and in between jovial exchanges of gossip we gaily pitched our junk. Late Sunday afternoon, the sky would haze over with smoke from the burning trash. And yet, be reasonable. Bedsprings and tin cans don't burn, nor green branches just cut from trees, nor wet garbage. The abyss grew shallower as the pile grew higher with every passing week, despite the burning, and then came the day the state outlawed open burning, so we began to bury the stuff under truckloads of dirt. Underground, without air or light, the town's discarded solids settled in, forming an archaeological goldmine. And the pile kept growing higher, the abyss shallower, until you could no longer pull your pick-up to the edge and toss stuff overboard. Now you had to pitch it up, and watch helplessly as it came rolling back down and landed at your feet. It smelled, too, and flies and gulls loved the place. But the state didn't. I think it was the junk mail proliferation of the 'eighties that finally did us in. The state closed our dump.

2.

As for me, I was deep into it long before the arrival of the natty little black bag. Nothing like coming to a wild piece of land with no established life-support systems—no toilet, no water supply, no power, no shelter, no phone, and no place to dump anything—to teach you the consequences of waste.

Our first object lesson: John, the big burly Italian guy who came with his backhoe and bulldozer to prepare our building site, was yanking cedar stumps out of the old cellarhole. Kal and I cringed at the gruesome din his machinery made as he wrenched rocks and roots like a diesel-powered Cuchulainn. We kept ourselves busy pulling up the milkweed stalks that hid the old spring someone told us was at the bottom of the field, when suddenly John came driving toward us with his big yellow bulldozer, pushing a load of ugly stumps with the blade.

"Where do you want these stumps?" he shouted over the fuming roar of his machine.

Kal and I looked at each other. Want these stumps? *We* didn't want these stumps. That's why we hired *John* to pull them out. You mean now we have to deal with them? You mean he won't just take them home with him at the end of the day? You mean we have to find a place on OUR LAND we'd be willing for him to destroy with his monstrous machine, leaving us with gouges in the wildflowers and an ugly pile of stumps that will never decompose in this century or the next?

3.

I am stooping, a figure in the twilight, by the edge of a one-lane dirt road. I walk here every day. I've grown keen at discriminating the proper from the improper, what lives here from what intrudes. Of course by now I include myself among what properly lives here, though by living here I've intruded upon the surrounding field and woods. Pheasants used to live in my old cellarhole, and whip-poor-wills up among the poplars and pines. Porcupines haven't yet heard that they are included in the category "intruder." They think I am. They think the plum trees I planted are theirs. Shows you how much they know.

I'm the one that knows. I walk briskly down the middle of the road until snapped to attention by a white styrofoam cup gleaming in the dusk among the glossy wintergreen shrubs. I know just what to do. I swoop, pluck, and deposit the intruder in the black bag I carry for this purpose. Then I continue on down the road without breaking stride. My practiced eye scans the bushes without forgetting to look up at the beautiful treetops aglow with the setting sun.

Whatever you do, don't let the litter get you down. Just do something about it. Do what little you can.

4.

Or maybe you want to do more. Clean up your whole town, for example. Somebody's got to do it, so here I am, scooping drenched bread bags from a flooded roadside ditch. Our volunteer crew spends a spring Saturday sorting what intrudes from what belongs. We could interpret barking dogs and people staring at us from behind their curtains as signs that we ourselves intrude, but we know what we're doing. We can't help their littered yards, but in the ditches we distinguish grass, violets and lilies from plastic, glass, paper, metal. Our black bags begin to bulge with soggy trash.

5.

Along this length of road the litter comes in waves. Here lives one who drinks malt liquor, and his neighbor favors whiskey. Their empties streak the roadside brand by brand, each toss a gesture toward immortality, which is more than I can hope for myself, despite my virtuous bagful. Grass will cover their bottles anyway, come summer, so why do I bother dragging this heavy black bag? And what will I do with it, come to think of it?

6.

Atop the ridge for which our town is famous, huge slabs of rock and blushing heath indent toward a jewel-like pond. We can see three or four ridges toward the coast, and another pond, and the white steeples of the village below. Why, I ask my fellow volunteers, why does the most beautiful spot attract the most slovenly show of trash? We pick broken glass off a granite ledge, and bottle caps and cigarette packs. We enter a blueberry field that sports hundreds of limp slush-cone containers hung from the reddening bushes like hankies left to dry in the sun. Does this spot mark the exact distance it takes to eat a slush-cone, as measured from the point of origin, the village store a mile below? Did one child on a bike do all this, or one adult in a car, tossing the evidence in the same spot time and again, a collection of stolen pleasures?

7.

I confess: I used to toss an apple core at the same turn every day, driving home from work. It was a ritual, like the slush-cones perhaps. It said, "Hello, deer, I'm home, and here's something for you!"

Apple cores are biodegradable, I told myself, food for the wildlife. Not to mention a harmless proof of my aim. But I won't do it again, now that I can picture some clean-up crew finding my half-rotted pile and wondering why.

8.

Is tossing trash from a moving vehicle an expression of joy, abandon, a hello to the environment? "Wheee! It's me-e!" Tantamount to writing a poem or bursting into song?

9.

No.

10.

But then, who's to say that humans are bad for littering the earth? Maybe those people with littered yards find the design as beautiful as a cluster of daffodils or a restored stone wall. If the natural order includes us, shouldn't it include what we fling as much as what we arrange? Aren't we dishonest to hide our leavings inside a black bag?

11.

Not that black plastic bags are innocent. They're made from oil, they degrade poorly when buried, they create toxic fumes when burned.

12.

Wonder what a blackbird would say about it?

Can't Get There from Here

1990

Trash is something you leave behind. A residue, evidence of your existence on this planet, your mark in history. If you live in a place, sooner or later personal responsibility will force you to deal with your own traces, or else the flies and seagulls and state regulators will. But a tourist can toss and move on, thinking all the while, Ah what lovely scenery, what a charming place, so quaint, so beautiful, so unspoiled.

Scenery is never enough for tourists, and trash is not their only mark on the history of this place. While the neon "Jesus Saves" was once the brightest thing on Route One in Rockland, now you can't even notice it for all the flashing "No Vacancy" signs and flapping flags of commerce. The sign's still shining, though, in competition with the golden arch of McDonald's where they tore down their building to put up a parking lot, then re-built bigger and better than ever next door. Along with commercial development—this in a town with homeless people and a failing fishing industry—comes traffic.

Tourists have traditionally made their way north through fish-smelling, working-class Rockland to get to Camden, the rich cousin just up the road. Before a single Rockland eatery ever hung a fern in the window, the plates of Camden's restaurants were already garnished with radicchio. But radicchio is never enough for tourists. Now the once-sleepy town of Rockland yawns and stretches awake, its "under-utilized" waterfront re-zoned to meet the upscale future. If you're going to put up with traffic problems, say the developers, you might as well cash in on those passing cars. You might just as well hang out your ferns, open your espresso bars, sell your T-shirts and plastic lobsters. When all is said and done, tourists bring in money and leave trash, but underneath it's still a story of roads.

I had thought trash was the real plot of the 'nineties, not tourism, not commerce, not roads. Maybe that's true in my small town where there's nothing but beauty for a tourist to want. I even thought trash might help us control tourism, if it should threaten our community, by employing this clever idea: that the Solid Waste Committe should merge with the Planning Board for their weekly meetings in the Town Hall, because the way I see it, it's in one end and out the other. The Planning Board is the intake valve, regulated by the enforcement of local development rules. The wider the opening in this regulatory valve, the greater volume of trash will issue forth for the Solid Waste Committee to deal with. If we can't even cope with our present trash, how can we possibly allow much in the way of new development, either housing or commercial? I propose that we close that valve down until we know what to do with the stuff that's pouring out the other end.

While waiting for the Town Selectmen to embrace my proposal, I devoted my positive energy to our new recycling efforts. But here's what happens when you're so busy bundling papers and hauling them off to the Town Hall parking lot for recycling that you don't have time to read them. One day, holding your thumb on the twine as you tie one off, you read: "LOCAL BYPASS ROUGHED OUT: OFFICIALS UNVEIL PRELIMINARY PLANS." All of a sudden you find that your coastal neighbors' problem with congested roads is about to supplant trash as your town's major issue.

Whenever I hear about "officials" making "plans," especially when those words occur in conjunction with "local," it's as if I'd been hit by a sudden swarm of mosquitoes. I begin to swat frantically at anything that whines until the palms of my hands are spotted with the blood of crushed insects, which just happens to be my blood. I quickly untie the bundling twine and take that issue off the recycling pile. I take it all the way back home, and up to the study. I uncover the old Smith Corona manual typewriter that my husband got for a Bar Mitzvah present in 1955, and wind in a piece of recycled stationery. The Smith Corona is the perfect model for cranky "Letters to the Editor," with e's just below the line and the dots on the i's making holes in the page, an occasional half-red letter when the black-and-red ribbon slips out of place.

This trusty machine has written its share of cranky letters, the most famous series being the one-sided conversation Kal carried on with the United States Postal Service over the closing of our beloved post office, another case of "officials" making "plans" for "locals." What happened there was that George retired and closed his store, and we suddenly found ourselves Zipless. Just put your regulation government mailboxes out by the side of the main road, the federal officials said, though how we were supposed to sink the regulation pole to the regulation depth in the frozen ground was not officially accounted for. Nor was the complex choice of delivery options ever officially explained to us locals. Our town, the name of which appeared on no Maine highway maps though it hung modestly over the TETLEY TEA sign at the store along with an official zip code, our town now ceased its official existence. And with its death came the ultimate civic identity crisis: we residents were faced with three possible towns to choose as an address. Already our phones were divided between two different exchanges so that a next-door neighbor might be a toll-call away, and Directory Assistance would find you untraceable on their computer time and again. Now no one even knew their neighbor's address anymore. "Where do you live?" would elicit answers like: my postal address is A, my street address is B, but my house is actually in C, even though my phone exchange is D. I suppose all this had the one advantage of making it even harder to track us down, if seclusion is what we want, which it is.

Kal rode the old Smith Corona as far as the State Postmaster General before realizing he was hopelessly mired in bureaucratic mud. Not until he called in the two United States Senators did he finally get the Postal Service to send out an official explanation to residents: we could use the old town name with the zip code of the newly adopted post office. After all that selfless work on Kal's part, we turn out to be the only ones in town who still use the old name. But I tell you, change comes hard to this ornery Smith Corona, and so it begins my first "Letter to the Editor" with a proud rendition of that old address.

First pausing to review the newspaper lying here beside me on the desk, I can see that while we struggled to keep our town's name, this article spells out a threat to much more:

... *studies of the Camden area, which is described in the report as having an "existing mobility deficiency" with speed "restricted to less than 50 m.p.h.," have shown that widening Route 1 is not feasible. "Travelling at 35 miles per hour is fine if you want to take the time to look around, ... but for the traveler who's going somewhere*

*and wants to get there, a four-lane highway with access limited . . .
is needed."* The bypass is being designed for this kind of motorist
. . . *although it is also expected that truck use will be considerable.*
And take a look at this map: here's the "hypothetical line" the
Department of Transportation has drawn for this new highway. It
would bring those fast cars and trucks right through our inland
jungle, where they apparently think it is "feasible" to pour on the
concrete. They mean to break up that summer traffic jam [mobil-
ity deficiency] at the stop sign in Camden if it takes thirty million
dollars to do it! Anything is better than a traffic light "where the
mountains meet the sea." A highway that takes tourism away from
the towns that depend on it, and through towns that won't benefit
in any way from it, now this is modern engineering at its best. So
much more cost-effective than funneling traffic onto existing roads
that already bypass parts of Route One, or designing some new
parking lots and one-way streets in town, or a couple of extra cops
to direct traffic on Main Street for those two months a year when
mobility reaches a critical deficiency. I'm no engineer, but they're
going to hear a thing or two about this from me! Me jungle native,
me no like asphalt.

I give the old Smith Corona a pat, and begin:

*A Route One bypass, such as the one "unveiled" last week, would
ruin the slow backwaters of Midcoast Maine, and for what? So
people can drive through the area so fast that they won't even see
what's been ruined: towns slashed in two by the fast-lane, land lost
to farms and homes, wildlife dispersed. These towns will bear the
burden of pollution, trash, and taxes that follows inevitably in the
wake of highways.*

(You know me, still clinging to that subplot— trash and taxes—
even in this story of roads.)

Of course, if we put in six lanes at Kittery—WELCOME TO MAINE: THE WAY LIFE SHOULD BE—I suppose we owe them highways enough once they get this far north. Hey, who is this bypass for, anyway? And who's paying for it? And who says so?

There, I feel a little better. But not all better. I begin a project of clipping all relevant news items from the two local papers, and start a file. The more I clip, the more the headlines seem to proliferate. Call it the scissors trick, it seems to be good for getting a local issue to coagulate.

ROUTE 1 BYPASS: DANGEROUS CURVES AHEAD.

ROUTE 1 BYPASS: AN IDEA GETS GOING.

THE BYPASS: WHAT WILL IT DO?

PROJECTIONS SHOW GROWTH FOR ROUTE 1 CORRIDOR COMMUNITIES.

And I begin to wonder if there are a lot of old Smith Coronas out there when I see "Letters to the Editor" with headings like:

Forewarned.

Doctor, Save My Heart: Who Needs This Bypass Anyway?

Bypass Wrong Fix.

Cape Cod North?

Ayuh, things are heating up in these inland parts. The jungle natives are getting restless. Now that we have a map with a real hyphothetical line on it, no one believes the Department of Transportation's reassuring denials. If there is no plan, the letters reiterate, then where did this line come from? And when are you going to ask us about using that "land out there," which one letter-writer says *happens to be part of my back yard!* And why is it that the Department of Transportation thinks it is the Department of *Highways?* There are more progressive ways to move people from here to there, like railroads for example. Aren't you worried about the greenhouse effect, or, more immediately relevant, the report that this county has worse air quality than some of the nation's biggest cities? And when are you going to take notice that the more highways you build, the more highways you need? *Crowds, traffic, inflated property values hurt the ones who can't bypass Camden—the residents. Why encourage even more traffic to pass through the state? To ruin more towns, and create the need to build more bypasses?*

Roads, and the prevention thereof, have clearly supplanted trash as the hot topic of the year. Some of the letters suggest alternatives to building another highway, and on this I have a few ideas myself. Heard the one about the drawbridge at Kittery? And then there's my proposed biomedical fix: inoculating all the natives and newcomers with that old Serum B, the blackfly venom that makes you immune to certain arguments. But my favorite idea is more realistic, I think. It creatively takes one problem and solves it by adding another. I personally think it's silly to build a bypass so people can avoid what they're coming here to see: the coast of Maine. The proposed bypass will take people through places they didn't even know were there to be seen, and in the process it will destroy those places. That just doesn't make any sense. But take the problem of high property values in Camden. Maybe we could kill two problems with one highway. Let me explain.

The State of Maine bases its aid to education on a town's assessment, so that the more valuable the town's property, the less help the town gets for school funding. So many people are beginning to recognize Camden as one of the prettiest and most desirable places to live, own a second home, or, increasingly, retire, that the people who've lived here all along find themselves paying higher and higher taxes on their home simply because somebody else wants it. And not only that, more and more of their tax dollar now goes to support the schools, which keep getting bigger and bigger. And since there are still all the other budget items to pay for, like the rising cost of dumping trash (don't forget), Camden faces a major financial crisis. So, my solution to this is let's cut a highway through the most expensive waterfront neighborhoods in Camden, which would immediately drop their valuations, thus qualifying Camden for a return to the level of state aid to education it used to enjoy. A side benefit would be that if we ran the highway right along the coast, we could all get a good look at Penobscot Bay as we whiz by at 50 miles per hour. I figure if we have to build new highways, we might as well get something for our tax dollars, don't you agree?

Now before you write me off as a lone victim of the NIMBY syndrome (Not In My Back Yard), I'd like to show you how my bulging file folder begins to change tone as the months go by. Headlines like these encourage me to continue my scisso-phrenic activity:

TOWNS FEEL BYPASSED BY PLANS FOR BYPASS.
BYPASS ALTERNATIVES OFFERED.
BYPASS NOT CAST IN ASPHALT.
HOPE SAYS 'NO' TO RTE. 1 BYPASS.

It finally took a town named Hope to lift us out of hopelessness. The Selectmen of this town bisected by the hypothetical line finally requested the Department of Transportation to meet with them, and then proceeded to invite citizens from all the surrounding towns to the meeting. It turned out to be THE big event of the year, bigger than the biggest Bean Supper ever held in these parts. Every car that turned off the main road that night was heading for the Hope School, with state police directing traffic, cars parked all over the playing field, video equipment in the classrooms for the overflow crowd. The air rumbled with excitement as 1,000 of us gathered for a re-run of the 'sixties. Long hair, long skirts, sandals, placards saying "Save it—Don't pave it!" A petition to the governor. T-shirts and bumper stickers for sale. There weren't any dogs, more people had short hair than long, the age range was wider. Instead of rock music, there was video recording equipment and TV news cameras, instead of marijuana there was lemonade. Most telling of all, we sat in rows on folding chairs in a school gym, we lined up at the microphone to speak. Thirty years later, "power to the people" had finally come of age, which only goes to support my claim that being 30 means you can DO something with your dream.

I know one thing the chief of the Department of Transportation (DOT) never dreamed, that he'd be up there on a dais facing 1,000 sharp critics in some little dot on the map he thought didn't know its bypass from its elbow. Or he did dream it, and it was a nightmare, because he ended up sending his assistant as the human sacrifice. And how does a bureaucrat deal with a thousand hostile natives whose major weapon against his word is their number? He begins by playing dumb. (The headline the next week that best captured the flavor of this tactic stated: *What, Me Bypass?*) Next, he attempts to lull them. (Headline: *No Lullaby This.*) Finally unable to avoid employing the logic of words, he offers reasons for the highway remedy. (*A Remedy for the Remedy.*) And in the end, frightened by the low roar of disapproval from the massed natives, he agrees with one of the election-year politicians in attendance that night. He confirms that *people can have an effect on what is planned and decided.*

And so it stands. No bypass. For now anyway.

If history is the story of human progress racing forward like a car on a highway, no wonder I wanted to live in a wild place where history came to die. Me no like asphalt. But the catch is, me drove here on asphalt, me cut down trees to build a house, me uprooted witchgrass in favor of beans. Me guilty of membership in this human "race." But Hope gave me hope: if progress is cyclical, not linear, then I can claim my part in the healing cycle. History didn't come here to die. It came to recover, and so did I.

Note: All quotations from the Camden Herald *and* Rockland Courier-Gazette, *November 1989 - May 1990.*

The Color Orange

1991

History will never die as long as there is language. And believe me, I know what I'm talking about because, be she mad or be she sane, she's a professor and language is her middle name.

Good trick, huh? See how a simple twist of language can separate me from myself and make "me" into "her"? One little switch puts a distance between the I who speaks and the she who's spoken of, a *subject* and an *object*. This detachment can come in handy when it leads to action, as human history shows all too well. You can't really blame humanity, though. It's not as if we consciously choose this act of linguistic definition. When it comes to the rules of syntax, it's Us or Them all the way.

I am describing nothing less than the condition of belonging to any culture. Even a chipmunk has a limited view of the universe, and it's not just because he never went to college. As for us verbal animals, we only see what culture gives us words for, and words lead to actions. Take the color orange as an example.

When I looked out the unfinished window of my new dining room and saw the blaze-orange surveyors' ribbons flapping from the trees across the road, I dropped my Exacto knife and began to roar like a lion. An objective viewer of this scene would be as puzzled by my outburst as Kal and Chris were until they saw the orange ribbons, too, and shared with their mad companion the fiercely territorial reaction. But you, the uninitiated viewer, what would you think? You might wonder why a perfectly lovely color would provoke such a primitive response, or how the very word "orange" had come to stand for the evils of development, operating as a kind of mysterious code-word. And you might even be moved to pity the otherwise innocent color for the cruel defamation heaped upon it by these savage jungle-dwellers.

I myself used to favor the color orange. Sunsets and citrus and maple leaves in autumn, tiger cats and orioles, pumpkins and carrots. And of course the color orange has saved my life every fall since I came to live in deer-hunting country, where a trip to haul water from the spring at the edge of the woods can be a life-threatening episode that even belting out "Amazing Grace" won't protect me from if I'm not also dressed from head to foot in bright orange gear. You never know. If it moves and it isn't orange, it might be a deer, even if it is singing "I'm not a deer! I'm not a deer!" at the top of its lungs, a trick the critters would do well to learn from Kal, who sings it desperately loud in the garden as he turns the compost heap one more time before the November frost comes down for good. They say deer are pretty smart. They also say hippies are pretty dumb, hauling water and all. That's one reason I finally gave it up. Didn't want the townsfolk to call me dumb behind my back, or shoot me in the back by accident.

All of which is just a long way of saying that I've finally seen the light—the orange light, which I've decided to re-define as a positive color. I figure if I can just replace the habitual negative reaction incited by those infernal orange ribbons, I'll be well on my way to recovery from the pain of development. I want to be a whole person again, not excluded from any part of the visual or emotional spectrum.

Exclusion is another thing that language is good at doing. You just have to read this book to see how many times I attempt to differentiate the acceptable from the unacceptable through a clever use of words. If it's in the ditch, it's trash; if it's in the bag, it's a recyclable. Or my preoccupation with defining a "native," or those rules that I believed could make developers really care about the land. I should know by now, with twenty years as a professor behind me and twenty to go, that words are only worth the paper they're written on. (Of course, paper is worth a lot these days, with the waning tree supply and all. But more of that later.)

Still, "do what I do, not what I say" is a better motto for country life. You can learn a lot from books, but watch how the guys at the feed store will chuckle if you tell them you followed the instructions in a book when it was time to skin your rabbits! Words and even illustrations are inadequate for describing exactly how to kill a rabbit quickly so it won't suffer. Words can never teach you how to lift a 4' x 8' sheet of plywood to your shoulders in a heavy wind as effectively as a demonstration from a friendly carpenter who's nice enough not to laugh as you get blown halfway down the driveway. Nor does the possession of a written deed mean you can "own" land, ever. But this gets into the tricky part.

Written words may not always be the best means of communication, but they do comprise the only legal means. When it comes to buying "real estate," you enter into a system of symbols on paper that has nothing real about it. What is a deed but a piece of paper purchased with another piece of paper called a check, backed up by pieces of paper called money, loaned to you by the bank when you handed over some collateral in the form of another piece of paper declaring that you own something worth the amount you want to borrow? You still don't "own" the land—the bank does—and you no longer "own" the collateral either. You don't own a damn thing until the paper tiger curls all the way around and swallows its own tail.

But even then, what does it mean to say "I own land"? "I" am the *subject*. What I "do" is the *verb*. Whom I do it "to" is the *object*. In the sentence "I own land," the syntax gives the privilege of action to "I" (the subject). "Land" (the object) doesn't do anything, except become owned. And because land has the status of a thing, I can be misled into assuming that land has no rights.

Or take the ungrammatical phrase "me jungle native, me no like asphalt." Such language, a common parody of "uncivilized" speech, portrays a speaker who mistakes herself for an object ("me"), a thing that is acted upon by an unnamed subject. This is the historic position of the exploited. How different to declare proudly, "I AM a jungle native, I DO NOT LIKE asphalt," where a subject stands up for her own identity and rights.

All this brings me back to my personal quest to re-define the color orange. If I'm going to own land, I want to minimize the colonial guilt. Tying orange ribbons around trees to mark the boundaries symbolizes a kind of ownership that leads too easily to exploitation. If I look out at those ribbons, and they demarcate an *object* I've paid good money for, I might just take my chainsaw to those woods in an effort to get something "off of it" for the money I put in. This is sensible economics, another language that gives the privilege of action to a *subject* with money, and makes anything of value into an *object*. Money talks, and the power of its language creates effects, in this case a cut-over piece of woods and the loss of habitat for thousands of "others" who talk funny, if at all.

The ability to create repercussions is one difference between the language of money and the language of the trees. Trees don't make things happen. Trees have to accept whatever happens. Their only weapon is growth, which works against them in making them an even more desirable commodity. Just think if money did grow on trees! Tree-farming would become the new stock exchange, and all the brokers would have to turn in their three-piece suits for a pair of overalls. This begins to sound vaguely like my plan to transform developers into good local citizens. But really, it is scarcity, not fecundity, that drives the economy, so I suppose organically-grown money would soon lose its value. Then they could go ahead and cut down trees just the same, and put on their pin-stripes to go to market. You can't win, if you're a tree.

In my attempt to reclaim the good color orange, I have realized that land and I are in this together—two subjects. TREES HAVE RIGHTS, just as I do. Biological life is not a commodity. It has no monetary value. It belongs intimately to itself. Orange ribbons don't make those trees into objects of mine, any more than a cat who pisses on your front steps becomes the owner of your house. If I insist on staking out my territory (and I'm not sure pissing on trees will do any good), I'll have to resort to my one advantage over the cat—language, and the Us-Them mentality that language supports. I will call these woods Mine. I will say Keep Out. And miraculously, in our human system, saying this gives me the legal right to protect my trees' rights. I sure hope they appreciate it.

Now let me tell you what I've done to mitigate the negative effects of human language and to renew the best of orange. I've taken to planting young trees on the "lot" we saved from the developer, and bedecking them with orange ribbons so I can find them as grass and goldenrod grow up zealously around them. No matter what language makes us believe, nature doesn't hand out special privileges. Saplings have no more right to live than milkweed. Everyone has to get along, or die out. So I figure there's nothing like a bunch of young trees to help me accept growth and change. I can't prevent the woods I don't "own" from resounding with the buzz of chainsaws and the banging of hammers. I can't keep people away forever, and I'm willing to concede I do have a decent crop of new neighbors on the other three "lots" we ended up with across the road. I suppose this admission is a sign of healing, but I wonder if it's dangerous just to accept change. The pain is healed over, but there are terrible scars. Now our ridge is no longer simply innocent woodland but a saleable commodity, something called "acreage." Now FOR SALE signs abound as other chunks of land are cut up, cut over, and put on the market. Now the local cash crop is money, which has a definite tendency to deplete the soil.

I have to accept change since I can't stop it, but I do exult in the row of hemlocks Kal fortuitously transplanted from the woods ten years ago to shield our house from the road. I festoon each one with orange ribbons as we move down the line pruning the growing tips with a vengeance, to make the bushes thick enough to block any sound except the warbling of song sparrows. I want these ribbons to stand for my commitment to the life of trees, and the beneficial relationship between humans and trees that Kal and I have entered into by living on this land. I want our son to grow up with trees. Noah and I took a step toward the future by planting a row of sugar maples to define the boundary of our new "lot," an orange ribbon flapping from each frail sapling crowned with a few tiny green leaves. From the road only the orange shows, but give these trees thirty years. Thirty years is long enough to make a dream happen. In thirty years, the trees and Noah will reach maturity, and I trust he'll be pouring maple syrup on his pancakes and calling it a good life, neighbors and all.

The Language of the Trees

1991

It's one thing to talk about healing, but it's another to live with the scars. Things haven't exactly gone the way we thought they would on this old backroad, where history is moving forward as surely as the seasons. As I walk my usual two miles up the ridge and down again under a canopy of leaves, I reflect on my bouts of madness that have finally given way to elegy. Maybe that's all insanity, or humor for that matter, really is, a protection from sadness that you can't fix. I've learned to count on wilderness to soothe me, but I fear that even my remedy is threatened. I walk, and the lush summer growth leans low over the narrow dirt road until I feel myself a small mass of life passing through a tunnel of other lives, all green and quiet except for the liquid rushing of leaves in the evening breeze.

This walk, this sense of living among other lives not human, gives substance to my life here. For all these years I've walked the ridge, passing under the shelter of these predictable limbs. At first I listened *to* the changing sounds, and now I listen *for* the sounds I've come to know by heart. Chickadees in winter, and the sighing of pines, the clatter of frozen branches. And then the robins, towhees, mourning doves, sparrows, finches, thrushes join in, come summer, and dappled sunlight dances on the ferns. Then back to just plain chickadees, grey-white-black like the branches that remain when the green drops off, like the lichen-covered boulders that were hidden under brush. And back and forth I walk under the rhythm of these changes from year to year, knowing my own small life as it passes through a tunnel of other lives.

But something has come to change those changes, something terrifying in its power to change change. Something I have to admit is kin of mine, for I am human in this tunnel of green, and only a guest here in these woods. It's taken me this long to confess that really I belong to that other family.

In the space of these familiar two miles, tonight I pass by four newly posted real estate signs gleaming pinkish-white in the dusk. They look odd in the tall tangle of green—FOR SALE—and within one summer week they are nearly overgrown with weeds. Nearly, but not quite. Nothing can stop them. Now the domain of these regal trees is marked and mapped, something to be bought, though they stand as straight and tall as ever. Trees can't read.

But I can. I belong to the human family and I speak its language. I know what's coming, even if the trees don't. I know they're worth money now, endangered by their own market value. Farther up the ridge, where no one lives but giant oaks and pines, I come upon a load of new gravel dumped on the ledgy road, and skidder tracks chewed into the mud, and the smell of engine grease. Limbs strewn every whichway, and shreds of leaves and bark, tell of a struggle in which the trees had nothing to say. Language is not one of their weapons. They have no defense against the oil-eating giant with chains on its feet that makes a clanging roar I can hear all the way down at my house. Tonight the skidder is parked under a big pine, its metallic hulk hardly silent, but at least not clanging. Tonight the woods are silent, and the ravaged debris whispers to me in the falling twilight, to the rhapsodic tune of a lone thrush.

I walk the length of rutted road, listening to the special language I've learned to understand in the years of walking this quiet path. It's a language whose syntax is breath, scent, light, dew. It's a language of the heart and senses, a language of consolation, of courage. Grief does not happen in this language, or anger, or madness. It's a language like that of an old grandmother who no longer speaks, but if you hold her cool, papery hand lightly in your own, you absorb the length of her days on earth, and you feel love, only love, with perhaps a tinge of your own sadness that is not her sadness. You long for her to tell you, something, some gem to guide you to your own more distant death, but all she tells you is Yes, Yes, her old pulse calm beneath the aged skin.

I find a little strip of bark fallen in the road. I pick it up and sniff its damp skin. It smells vaguely of bar-and-chain oil. I sense that I am holding the evidence of some violent crime I am powerless to prevent. I desperately want to protect these trees. Their living supports the life of everything else on this ridge, even my own. And standing here amid this indelicate equipment, I acknowledge that in other ways their living also supports the life of those who cut them down.

They come, armed with chainsaws, cherry-pickers, skidders, bulldozers. They come, and take whatever they find, except the sky. The trouble is, they take much more than they know they are taking. Certainly they take the trees, big old ones for lumber, smaller ones for firewood or pulp. They take the stone walls on their next trip, not doing anyone any good up here. The unwanted rubble that Zebediah and his brothers turned into borders of beauty, an enduring tribute to their labor, will bring a good price in town where elegant stone walls denote wealth. They even take the top-soil, but this they don't know they are taking. They don't know what soil is worth, a thousand years of rot that will soon run down off the treeless ridge to clog the lovely stream in the valley. And there, once again without knowing it, they will take the lives of ducks, geese, moose, beaver, deer, fish, who can't live with topsoil in their water. And they will take, also without ever knowing it, the quiet language of wilderness. They will teach the land to speak in neighborhood tongues, the cries of children, the slamming of screen doors, the whirr of lawnmowers, the choking of cars.

I admit by now that I came here, too, adding my own human life sounds to the call of the whip-poor-will, woodcock, and grouse. I swore to live an honest life, but I could have settled here even without that promise, and the whip-poor-will and I would be the only ones to say if I've been true to it. People have to live some-where, and I am people too. Once the trees are gone and the profit made, the land will still be here, FOR SALE, someplace to call home. Am I really any less an intruder just because Kal and I brought our own compost to this place where nothing human had happened for a century, this place no one but we knew was worth anything? We were willing students of this wild place, becoming small in its shadow, always looking up, always listening. The land will still be here, but once the woods are gone, how will the new neighbors learn to speak the language of the trees? Who will teach them to plant again?

It's nearly dark now. I turn around and head down the ridge, past a huge stack of long oaks lying on their side, long, not tall as they were grown. I touch the length of them, and put my nose to the fresh cuts at the end of the logs. I wish them happiness as a floor, a table, a boat. I hear them whisper a thin "Good-bye . . ." and then I listen again in the blue-green dark, hoping they will point me into the future, as they have guided me to health in the past. I stand still in the road, breathing in their sharp scent, and then at last, when I am quiet enough, I hear their final message. "So it is . . . So it is . . . ," they say. And the voice trails off, like that of a dying grandmother, and I am the one left here grieving.

Epilogue

Outstanding in Her Swamp

1996

Where did you expect to find me, this winter of my 49th year? Life led me here, to stand alone on snowshoes in the blazing white light of a frozen beaver swamp, reading wind-etchings of bleached grass on the snow.

I place my shadow here among dead cedar trunks, some pointing a quizzical finger at the wide blue sky, some tipped over with black root-mass jutting above the snow, some arrested by my presence in their process of falling, slowly, when no one's here to watch. Today the brilliant sun makes me squint, begs my eyes to seek the cool dark hemlocks at the margin. Other days I come, zipped to the nose inside my parka, and let the wind blow snow obliquely across my eyes that watch the leaning ones resume their diagonal dance, perchance to fall.

When I am here no one is here. I cease. Behind me, my snowshoe tracks lead to this spot like the sure opening lines of a masterpiece, and then stop in the middle. For as long as my breath joins the breath of the swamp and rises as frosty steam above stiff cattails and swishing grasses, only the raven reads me, *rook-rook,* circling overhead, or bald eagle pointing a pencil-yellow beak at me from high in a cobalt sky. Ahead of me is trackless, the next thing, waiting. I stand planted here.

This frozen place looks dead but isn't. There is a history here that won't die as long as there is water. This old place was once a young and verdant stand of cedars, then flooded by beavers' drive to build and multiply, now crosshatched with tumbling silver trunks and reeds. But under the falling, finishing dance of the swamp lies the sponge, like a trust that endows nature with the means to go on living.

I stand upon this treasure, exposed in the middle of this frozen bog, invisible to all but raven, eagle, beaver, or any other breathing presence, cedar or balsam or you, reading me. Behind me, what led here. Ahead of me, blank. My middle is my beginning. I set off, eyebrows fuzzed with frost, into the rest of it.

Dear Reader,

In purchasing a copy of *Carrying Water as a Way of Life*, you have lent a hand in the do-it-yourself lifestyle the book describes. As with anything worthwhile—be it building, gardening, writing, or getting your words out to the people who want to hear them—I've learned you have to dedicate time, money, and attention to make it what you want. The founding of About Time Press and the publication of this book represent my commitment to that ideal.

To order *Carrying Water as a Way of Life*, send $9.95 ($10.50 in Maine). Please include shipping fee: $2.50 for 1–2 copies; $3.50 for 3–4 copies; 5–8 books no charge.

Ask us about bookstore, library, school, and quantity (9+) discounts.

Carrying Water is also available at bookstores and through Maine Writers & Publishers Alliance and national distributors. Please suggest it to your local bookseller or librarian. I thank you for reading this book, and welcome letters of response, invitations to speak or read, suggestions for future publications, and additions to our mailing list.

About Time Press
1050 Guinea Ridge Road
Appleton, Maine 04862
207-785-4634

THANK YOU FOR SUPPORTING THIS SMALL PRESS!